Modern English Fairy Tales
― 現代の英語おとぎ話 ―

編・著　西田　一弘
著　　Lena Clem
著　　岸上　英幹

ふくろう出版

Modern English Fairy Tales
－ 現代の英語おとぎ話 －

はじめに

I have seen with my own eyes the sibyl hanging in a jar, and when the boys asked her, "What do you want?" she answered, "I want to die."

　かつて私はこの目で、吊るした壺に入りこんでいる巫女を見たことがある、そして少年達が、「何が欲しい？」と尋ねると、彼女は答えた、「もう死にたいんだよ。」

　上記の文はアメリカの詩人 T.S. Eliot が The Waste Land『荒地』という詩集の巻頭言に書いたものである。Eliot は従来の湖畔詩人たちが４月を「花が咲き始め、若葉が芽吹き、明るく、希望に満ちた月」とうたっていた頃、彼は「４月は残酷な月だ」から始まる『荒地』を発表した。この書きだしは、その文字だけを見ていると矛盾に思えるかも知れないが、実は矛盾でないことが最後まで読むと分かるのである。これは彼独特のレトリックと言えよう。
　それゆえ、上記の「巫女の話」にも前提となる背景があるのである。エリオットは書いていないが、実はここに描かれている巫女はかつて、神様から、「あなたの望むものを一つあげるとしたら、何が欲しいか」と尋ねられ、巫女は「永遠の生命を！」と願ったのである。神は巫女の願いをかなえ、巫女はいくら年をとっても死ねないのである。
　この話を読むとき、私には一つの教訓が浮かんでくる。私たちが文章を読むとき、その表面に現れる文字だけを見ていてはいけないということである。文の奥には隠された意味があるかもしれない。多くがデジタル化されている時代にこそ、本書に表されて

いる Fairy Tales の心を読み取っていただければ幸いです。
　なお、本書に掲載されている頻出で重要な「前置詞」、「句動詞」の学習を本書のリーディングと合わせて行うと、英語リーディング力の向上に大いに役立つはずです。

Contents

はじめに
本書の使い方

UNIT 1　Modern English Fairy Tales ― 現代の英語おとぎ話 ―
- The Farmer's Daughter --- 10
- The Spoiled Child -- 18
- From Stars -- 23
- The Gold Coin -- 31
- The Gift --- 41
- The Fox and the Rabbit --- 46
- Trees --- 59
- From the Future -- 66

UNIT 2　GRAMMAR

Part 1　Understanding Prepositions ― 前置詞の理解 ―
Ⅰ．前置詞とは？ --- 82
Ⅱ．前置詞 "at" と "in" のイメージの違い --------------------------- 82
Ⅲ．前置詞 "until (till)" と "by" のイメージ ------------------------- 83
Ⅳ．前置詞 "up" のイメージ -- 84
Ⅴ．前置詞 "for" のイメージ --- 85
Ⅵ．前置詞 "from" と "since" のイメージ ---------------------------- 87
Ⅶ．前置詞 "with" のイメージ --- 88
Ⅷ．前置詞 "behind" と "beyond" のイメージ ----------------------- 89
Ⅸ．前置詞 "in" と "into" のイメージ --------------------------------- 90

Ⅹ．前置詞 "above" と "below" のイメージ ―――――――――― 91
Ⅺ．前置詞 "over" と "under" のイメージ ―――――――――― 91
Ⅻ．前置詞 "on" と "over" のイメージ ――――――――――― 92

Part 2　Understanding Phrasal Verbs ― 句動詞の理解 ―
Ⅰ．句動詞とは？ ――――――――――――――――――――― 96
Ⅱ．句動詞の基本概念 ――――――――――――――――――― 96
Ⅲ．「句動詞」の実際
　　　― Go, Come, Put, Run, Speak, Talk, Say, Tell, Look,
　　　Get, Call, Bring ― ―――――――――――――――― 102
　◎　基本動詞 "Go" ―――――――――――――――――― 102
　◎　基本動詞 "Come" ―――――――――――――――― 105
　◎　基本動詞 "Put" ――――――――――――――――― 108
　◎　基本動詞 "Run" ――――――――――――――――― 111
　◎　基本動詞 "Speak, Talk, Say, Tell" ――――――――― 115
　◎　基本動詞 "Look" ―――――――――――――――― 119
　◎　基本動詞 "Get" ――――――――――――――――― 121
　◎　基本動詞 "Call" ――――――――――――――――― 125
　◎　基本動詞 "Bring" ―――――――――――――――― 127
Ⅳ．基本動詞を含む重要な句動詞／熟語 ――――――――――― 131
Ⅴ．句動詞によく使用される基本動詞 ―――――――――――― 136

あとがき

本書の使い方

Unit 1　Modern English Fairy Tales
　― 現代の英語おとぎ話 ―

　英語を日本語を介さずに理解すること、即ちポイントとなる、Who（Whom）、When、Where、What、How、Why を意識して、リーディングを行うことが大切です。本書では、英語を英語で理解するように、英語の説明は英語でしてあります。大まかな意味をつかむようにしてください。物語の最後には5つのQUESTIONSがあります。その解答がわかること、解答を出せることが物語を理解していること、物語をもとに自分の考え方を構築していることになります。

　物語の内容は、概して徐々に難しくなっていますが、短い物語ですから、何回も読んで、物語の内容を理解すると共に、英語表現、英語圏の人々の考え方、英語の世界を味わってください。

　以下のURLを使用してインターネット上のYouTubeで、ネイティブ教員による本書の8つの物語の英語音声を聞くことができます。英語の発音とリズムを合わせて味わってください。

　　　http://eddykn.web.fc2.com　　　Good Luck Studying!!

Unit 2　Grammar

　Unit 2 Grammar では、Part 1 で前置詞を、Part 2 で句動詞を学んでください。共に、英語における頻出かつ極めて重要な学習事項です。Part 2 の句動詞には、練習のための問題もあり、さらに基本動詞を含む句動詞／熟語がまとめてあります。十分に活用してください。

・**本書で使用されている記号**

　　ⓝ　＝　名詞　　　ⓥ　＝　動詞　　　ⓐᵤₓ　＝　助動詞
　　ⓐ　＝　形容詞　　ⓐdv　＝　副詞　　ⓟrep　＝　前置詞
　ⓒonj　＝　接続詞　　ⓘnt　＝　間投詞　ⓟron　＝　代名詞

UNIT 1
Modern English Fairy Tales
― 現代の英語おとぎ話 ―

UNIT 1　Modern English Fairy Tales

The Farmer's Daughter

　　There was once a girl who knew nothing. As in knowing nothing, she knew everything about nothing. Her life was a simple one, a clean one. Almost one of the perfect lives. At least that was what she had always dreamed of, to be a princess in the land of dreams where there was nothing around to **cause** a **frown**. There lived a happy, rich little girl who had not a **care** in the world.

　　The reality was that she was a farm girl. Her mother had **passed away** a year **prior**, **along with** the money she brought in from her little shop in the city. Her father was a **lowly** farmer who worked hard in the **soil** day after day.

---

cause　ⓥ　to make something happen, especially something bad or unpleasant
frown　ⓝ　a serious, angry or worried expression on a person's face that causes lines on their forehead
care　ⓝ　a feeling of worry or anxiety; something that causes problems or anxiety
pass away　　to die
prior　ⓐ　happening or existing before something else or before a particular time
along with　　in addition to somebody/something; in the same way as somebody/something
lowly　ⓐ　low in status or importance
soil　ⓝ　the top layer of the earth in which plants, trees, etc. grow

The Farmer's Daughter

The year's harvest was cruel, and the crops would not grow. Her father struggled to raise even the smallest potatoes. It seemed the family would not last much longer. Her father's health was fading, and she, barely of birthing age, was too young to really take care of him.

Every day was the same routine. Wake up and work in the fields, make soup for her and her father, bathe, and sleep. It would repeat. Never-ending.

However, late at night, in her linens, the girl would sneak away to the outside world. From her breaking home, and behind the farmhouse, through the leaves and twigs and puddles of mud, deep, deep, deep into the darkness of the forest she went. In this darkness, the sounds of rushing water could quietly be heard.

---

raise (v)   to grow, especially in quantity; cultivate
last (v)   to survive something or manage to stay in the same situation, despite difficulties
fading (fade) (v)   to lose strength or vitality; wane
barely (adv)   in a way that is just possible but only with difficulty
birthing (a)   the action or process of giving birth
linen (n)   a type of cloth made from flax (= a plant with blue flowers), used to make high-quality clothes, sheets, etc.
sneak (v)   to go somewhere secretly, trying to avoid being seen
twig (n)   a small very thin branch that grows out of a larger branch on a bush or tree
puddle (n)   a small amount of water or other liquid, especially rain, that has collected in one place on the ground
rush (v)   to move or to do something with great speed, often too fast

UNIT 1 Modern English Fairy Tales

She had once heard her mother speak of a beautiful and handsome man from the forest by a small stream. This man, she had claimed, had rescued her from a wild beast when returning home on a detoured route from the city after having gotten lost.

Ever since then, she would hear the tales of this man. How his emerald-green eyes stood out strikingly against his elaborate, ancient attire. His ears were as sharp as the sword situated at his side. He wore armor upon his breast and calves, and shining gauntlets protected his forearms.

---

claim (v) to say that something is true although it has not been proved and other people may not believe it

detour (v) to take a longer route in order to avoid a problem or to visit a place; to make somebody / something take a longer route

tale (n) a story created using the imagination, especially one that is full of action and adventure

stood (stand) out to be easily seen; to be noticeable

elaborate (a) very complicated and detailed; carefully prepared and organized

attire (n) clothes

sword (n) a weapon with a long metal blade and a handle

situated (a) in a particular place or position

armor (n) special metal clothing that soldiers wore in the past to protect their bodies while fighting

calves (calf) (n) the back part of the leg between the ankle and the knee

gauntlet (n) a metal glove worn as part of a suit of armor by soldiers in the Middle Ages

forearm (n) the part of the arm between the elbow and the wrist

But he was a gentle man, claimed her mother.

One night, after returning home from the city, her mother exclaimed excitedly about how she was going to see the man again. That she had called to him for help with the shop.

It was not long before the woman fell ill. Doctors told how they could do nothing for her ailments. And then, soon after, the girl watched as her mother passed. But as she died, her hand had been outstretched, as though there was someone else there.

The shop gained a new owner, and the owner became the richest merchant in the land. Since then, the girl would escape to the forest, to the place by the little stream where her mother had told countless stories, and she would sit there. Sometimes, she would sing or play her little wooden flute, not expecting anything in return. But tonight, it was different. Her father needed her if he were to survive that night.

As a girl of barely birthing age, she could not physically help him with the chores that were needed to be done in the home. So, she did as her mother had done. She prayed.

---

exclaim (v)   to say something suddenly and loudly, especially because of strong emotion or pain

ailment (n)   an illness that is not very serious

pass (v)   to die; pass away

outstretched (a)   fully extended especially in length   (outstretch = to extend or expand; stretch out)

as though   in a way that suggests something

countless (a)   very many; too many to be counted or mentioned

chore (n)   a task that you do regularly

UNIT 1 Modern English Fairy Tales

"Please," begged the girl, with her knees in the waters of the small stream, "the crops are dead. My father is dying. I have nothing to offer, but someone please help."

There was no sound. There was no answer. Only silence. In desperation, the girl wailed, "I would give you anything I have to give, if you would only help my father!"

There was a glow, and something soft touched her shoulder. A man, of huge stature, kneeled to her. He had long, curly blonde hair that cascaded gracefully around his shoulders. She stared into those green eyes, as green and deep as emeralds. And those ears as sharp as the sword on his belt.

---

crop (n) a plant that is grown in large quantities, especially as food
desperation (n) the state of feeling or showing that you have little hope and are ready to do anything without worrying about danger to yourself or others
wail (v) to make a long, loud, high cry because you are sad or in pain
glow (n) a dull steady light, especially from a fire that has stopped producing flames
stature (n) a person's height
cascade (v) to fall or hang in large amounts

The Farmer's Daughter

She felt no fear, finding some form of comfort in those eyes. They were emeralds that offered security and an eternity of embrace. He held his free hand out to her, and she took it without hesitation.

Morning came, and the father rose to begin working. He felt rested, and went upstairs to wake his child.

She was not there.

In a panic, he ran outside to search the forests, but stopped when he saw the fields.

There, in front of his eyes, potatoes grew. Potatoes and tomatoes as large as human heads were suddenly fresh and ready for picking and eating. There were some goats, though he could not remember any; there were most certainly real, live goats. They appeared fresh for milking.

But, no matter how much the father searched, he never found his daughter. However, for the rest of the years of his life, his crops were the best in the land, and on his crops, he became rich. He could feed himself. He could fix the broken farmhouse. He was the most famous farmer in the land.

, finding   because she found

offer   ⓥ   to make something available or to provide the opportunity for something

eternity   ⓝ   a period of time that seems to be very long or to never end

embrace   ⓝ   an act of holding close with the arms, usually as an expression of affection; a hug

rested   ⓐ   feeling healthy and full of energy because you have had a rest or a period of relaxing, sleeping or doing nothing

feed   ⓥ   to give food to a person or an animal

UNIT 1　Modern English Fairy Tales

But once a year, when his crops were in full bloom and ready to be harvested, he could hear singing from the forest, accompanied by the sound of a flute. And every year on this day, he would sit by the small stream in the forest, and he would imagine his little girl as a princess, in the land of dreams, playing her flute and singing to his wife's ethereal man.

---

in full bloom　　　fully grown
accompanied (accompany)　　ⓥ　　to happen or appear with something else
ethereal　　ⓐ　　extremely delicate and light; seeming to belong to another, more spiritual, world

The Farmer's Daughter

QUESTIONS Answer the following questions in English.

1. What does "the man from the forest" look like?

2. What is the significance of the mother in this story?

3. Do you think that the farmer was selfish? Why do you think so?

4. Describe the character of the farmer's daughter.

5. What do you think happened to the farmer's daughter at the end of the story?

UNIT 1 Modern English Fairy Tales

The Spoiled Child

Once, long ago but not too long ago, there lived a spoiled little boy and his mother. He would always get what he wanted, and always did he tremble with rottenness when he did not. If his mother refused even the tiniest bit of anything, then the horrid boy would throw a mighty fit. Always he would get what he wanted.

One day close to the village of Samhaine, his mother became fed up with the wretched child, and gave him a fair warning.

"If you do not stop being so ungrateful, Child, then the goblins will crawl down the chimney and take you away!"

---

did (do) (aux) used when no other auxiliary verb is present, to emphasize what you are saying

tremble (v) to shake in a way that you can not control, especially because you are very nervous, excited, frightened, etc.

rottenness (n) the state of being very bad or disobedient

horrid (a) very unpleasant or unkind

mighty (a) very strong and powerful

fit (n) a short period of very strong feeling (throw a fit: to be very shocked, upset, or angry)

fed up tired; bored and annoyed (feed : to satisfy a need, desire, etc. and keep it strong)

wretched (a) used to show that you think that somebody/something is extremely annoying

fair (a) acceptable and appropriate in a particular situation

goblin (n) a small ugly creature that likes to trick people or cause trouble

The Spoiled Child

But the boy pointed and laughed at his mother, claiming falsity to her words and carrying on his path of terror.

Perhaps but a few nights after, or a few months, the boy had a mighty fit, for he did not want to eat his dinner. But his mother forced him to eat, and he spit it back at her.

"I do not want this disgusting morsel!" He screamed, tossing his limbs to the floor in a rage. Once more, his mother warned, "If you do not stop being so wicked, Child, then the goblins will crawl down the chimney and take you away!"

But once again, the boy pointed and laughed, calling to his mother an old hag and carrying on his path of terror.

Not a day later, again the boy found something to throw a fit about, and the mother warned him firmly.

, claiming		and he claimed / while he was claiming
falsity	(n)	the state of not being true or genuine
carrying on (carry on)		to continue doing something
path	(n)	a course of action, conduct, or procedure
fit	(n)	a sudden attack of an illness
for	(conj)	because
morsel	(n)	a small amount or a piece of something, especially food
limb	(n)	an arm or a leg; a similar part of an animal, such as a wing
rage	(n)	a feeling of violent anger that is difficult to control
point	(v)	to direct attention or indicate position with or as if with the finger
hag	(n)	an ugly and/or unpleasant old woman

UNIT 1 Modern English Fairy Tales

"If you do not stop being so horrid a child, the goblins will crawl down the chimney and gobble you up!"

When the boy did not heed her words of warning, but laughed and pointed, the mother huffed and said, "This shall be no fault of mine! This shall be a blessing!"

That night, as the boy snuck to the small kitchen to steal a morsel of food, he heard something amiss from the black of the chimney. Scared, the boy went to see what it was, but found nothing except a few ashes, and he laughed.

"Ha! Silly old hag! She does not know what she is talking about. No, she does not!"

And he carried on into the kitchen.

But before he could return, there was a cackle from the chimney, and a disfigured creature appeared, and the boy was swiftly gobbled up.

---

gobble ~ (up) ⓥ   to eat something very fast, in a way that people consider rude or greedy
heed ⓥ   to pay careful attention to somebody's advice or warning
huff ⓥ   to say something or make a noise in a way that shows you are offended or annoyed
snuck (sneak) ⓥ   to go somewhere secretly, trying to avoid being seen
amiss ⓐ   wrong; not as it should be
Scared,   As he was scared,
cackle ⓝ   a loud unpleasant laugh
disfigured ⓐ   having the appearance spoiled or ugly

When the mother rose from her sleep the next morn, she noticed the peace and quiet, and the mother blissfully rested.

"Alas! What a blessing it is, indeed."

---

morn (n) morning
blissfully (adv) in an extremely happy way
rest (v) to relax
alas (int) used to express sorrow, regret, grief, compassion, or apprehension of danger or evil
blessing (n) a favor or gift bestowed by God, thereby bringing happiness

UNIT 1 Modern English Fairy Tales

QUESTIONS   Answer the following questions in English.

1. Do you think that the child deserved to be gobbled up at the end? Why do you think so?

2. Do you think that the mother's reaction at the end is reasonable? Why do you think so?

3. Do you think it is the mother's responsibility that her child was spoiled and died? Why do you think so?

4. What do you think the lesson of this story is?

5. Why do you think that the use of fear and monsters is common in old fairy tales to teach children right from wrong?

From Stars

Once, long ago in a far away land, a land of seas and vast emptiness, a young girl of birthing age stumbled upon a simple pebble along the shores of the sea.

There was a lovely engraving scratched almost hastily into the crevices, which made it quite difficult to read what seemed like the letters "AT" in the shape of a heart. The young girl marveled at the interesting find , wondering what story lay behind the initials.

---

birthing (n)   the action or process of giving birth
stumbled (stumble) upon   to find something by chance or unintentionally
pebble (n)   a smooth, round stone that is found in or near water
shore (n)   the land along the edge of the sea or ocean, a lake or another large area of water
engraving (n)   a picture made by cutting a design into a piece of metal or another hard object
scratched (scratch) (v)   to damage the surface of something, especially by accident, by making thin shallow marks on it
crevice (n)   a narrow crack or break in a rock or wall
, which   and it
letter (n)   a written or printed sign representing a sound used in speech
marvel (v)   to be very surprised or impressed by something
find (n)   a thing or person that has been found, especially one that is interesting, valuable or useful
, wondering   and she wondered/while she was wondering
lay (lie) (v)   to be, remain or be kept in a particular state
   (lie behind ~ : to be the real reason for something, often hidden)

UNIT 1 Modern English Fairy Tales

Perhaps it was a star-crossed story in which the lovers died together, in each other's arms with the hope that they would be together forever!? Perhaps maybe it was a wonderful "happily-ever-after" story, and the two got married and had children!?

The young girl's eyes widened, her imagination becoming powerful as it got away from her.

A man with a beautiful face, beautiful green eyes, and curly red hair approached a curvy woman. It was immediate love at first sight, and the two fell into each other's arms. Although they were not supposed to be together, both being engaged to other people, they still sought out the arms of the other without paying any regard to their families' desires.

---

star-crossed ⓐ not able to be happy because of bad luck or fate
widen ⓥ to become larger in degree or range
, her imagination becoming and her imagination became
as ⓒᴏɴᴊ while something else is happening
got (get) away from to break loose and leave suddenly from
curvy ⓐ (of a woman's body) having large breasts and pleasing curves
immediate ⓐ happening or done without delay
sought (seek) out to look for and find somebody/something, especially when this means using a lot of effort
regard ⓝ attention to or thought and care for somebody/something

Together, forever to embezzle their love in time, they etched their initials in the pebble, tossing it out to sea in hopes that someone would remember them and their story.

Perhaps, the girl thought, the lovers had a struggle to be with each other, ending in a tragic romance where both of them should die. Or maybe, they both had the approval of their parents and they lived happily-ever-after in the end? Happily-ever-after with marriage and a family was everything a couple could ever dream of.

There was a sea of wondrous stories that passed through the curious eyes of the little girl, and she let a small smile cross her face as she slowly tucked the marred pebble into her pocket for safekeeping.

---

embezzle (v) to steal something, especially money

in time after a period of time when a situation has changed; time can become a hiding place in the context

etch (v) to cut lines into a piece of glass, metal, etc. in order to make words or a picture

tossing (toss) out to throw or cast away

approval (n) the action of accepting something

wondrous (a) strange, beautiful and impressive

tuck (v) to put something into a small space, especially to hide it or keep it safe or comfortable

marred (mar) (v) to damage or spoil something good

safekeeping (n) the fact of something being in a safe place where it will not be lost or damaged

UNIT 1 Modern English Fairy Tales

As she walked on her journey home in this vast, empty land of seas, the little girl hummed a tune unknown to anyone but her.

It wasn't until she passed by a large set of sea stones that she noticed the boy sitting at the edge of one of the bigger ones, his stony gaze taking in the endless wall of water.

"Hello. Haven't seen you around before," she said as she smiled at the boy. He turned his head towards her to take in her presence, returning the smile. Sharp, pointed ears stuck out from his red curly hair.

This struck the girl as strange.

---

vast ⓐ   extremely large in area, size, amount, etc.
hum ⓥ   to sing a tune with your lips closed
but ⓟⓡⓔⓟ   except; apart from
pass by   to go past
edge ⓝ   the outside limit of an object, a surface or an area; the part furthest from the centre
stony ⓐ   showing a lack of feeling or sympathy
gaze ⓝ   a long steady look at somebody/something
taking (take) in   to absorb something into the body, for example by breathing or swallowing
take in   to take notice of something with your eyes
presence ⓝ   the fact of being in a particular place
, returning   and he returned
pointed ⓐ   having a sharp end
stuck (stick) out   to be further out than something else or come through a hole
struck (strike) ⓥ   to come into somebody's mind suddenly

"I have not been here, lass. Why are you wandering alone? There could be something dangerous lurking out here. You could get hurt."

He moved from the rock easily, coming to stand before her. He was a good head taller than her.

"There's not another single person on this island. Just me. It is strange to see you around. Where'd you come from?"

The young boy merely pointed towards the sea.

"That way. I lost a pebble and came looking. Have you seen it? My pebble, I mean."

The young girl put her hand in her pocket, taking out the pebble with the initials.

"Just this, here. But I don't know if it is yours or not."

She noticed the boy's green eyes creased in a smile.

---

lass (n) a girl; a young woman
wander (v) to walk slowly around or to a place, often without any particular sense of purpose or direction
lurk (v) to wait somewhere secretly, especially because you are going to do something bad or illegal
where'd where did
merely (adv) used meaning 'only' or 'simply' to emphasize a fact or something that you are saying
point (v) to stretch out your finger or something held in your hand towards somebody/something in order to show somebody where a person or thing is
I mean used to explain or correct what you have just said
crease (v) to make lines in the skin; to develop lines in the skin

UNIT 1 Modern English Fairy Tales

He laughed happily as his eyes glittered with recognition.

"That'd be it. And looks like I've found the person I was looking for too!"

He took a finger and pointed it at her.

She tilted her head in confusion as the boy ruffled her hair. She protested, and fixed it. Her hair was a mess of curls, and they were hard to contain sometimes.

"This is us," he said excitedly as he pointed a long, slender finger at the pebble.

"Long ago. But now we're together again. Let's go home."

As the boy placed a sweet kiss on the girl's forehead, he took her hand. The young girl, through her confusion, looked to him in wonder as he dragged her out to sea.

---

as (conj) while something else is happening

glitter (v) to shine brightly with a particular emotion, usually a strong one

recognition (n) the act of remembering who somebody is when you see them, or of identifying what something is

that'd that would

tilt (v) to move, or make something move, into a position with one side or end higher than the other

ruffle (v) to disturb the smooth surface of something, so that it is not even

protest (v) to say or do something to show that you disagree with or disapprove of something, especially publicly

a mess of a lot of, many/much

contain (v) to prevent something from spreading or getting bad

forehead (n) the part of the face above the eyes and below the hair

dragged (drag) (v) to pull somebody/something along with effort and difficulty

They went under, and he showed her marvelous things. He showed her a kingdom where magical beings ruled. He showed her things he could do for her, and what he could give her.

The boy told her the story of the past: how the two of them were once together, and how she was a beautiful, curvy woman with long red curls. That he was a beautiful man with emerald green eyes and curly red hair.

She was interested, very interested in the story. She soon came to remember all of her memories of the pebble and the handsome man.

And in this sea, the young girl became a beautiful, curvy woman with long, red curls, and he became a beautiful man with emerald green eyes and curly red hair.

Without hesitation, they got married, and together they lived forever under the sea in a beautiful kingdom with the many magical beings that ruled there.

---

kingdom ⓝ a country ruled by a king or queen

being ⓝ a living creature

rule ⓥ to control and have authority over a country, a group of people, etc.

that ⓒⓞⓝⓙ used after some verbs, adjectives and nouns to introduce a new part of the sentence

came (come) to to reach a point where you realize, understand or believe something

UNIT 1   Modern English Fairy Tales

QUESTIONS   Answer the following questions in English.

1. What is the meaning of the title "From Stars"?

2. What were the young girl's two ideas about the pebble's story?

3. How did the boy look when the girl first met him?

4. Where did the boy take the girl?

5. What do the letters "AT" engraved in the pebble she found along the shores represent?

The Gold Coin

In a forest, far from the villages, much farther from the city, but not too far from the ocean, there lived an old man, his wife and their good daughter. They were very poor, and could not afford anything more than a small wooded hut and a little garden, and could barely afford to eat. Because they had so little, they were extremely grateful for everything they had. They knew it would be all they could ever have.

So, every morning and every evening, the wife would go out and tend to her little garden in front of their little hut. She loved this garden dearly, therefore she made good and sure to care for it.

One evening, the old wife went out to her garden and did her nightly routine, making sure the weeds were pulled and the flowers were watered and the soil was at its best.

---

hut (n) a small, simply built house or shelter

barely (adv) in a way that is just possible but only with difficulty

tend to to look after/take care of somebody who is sick, very old, very young, etc.

made (make) sure to do something in order to be certain that something else happens

good and very

care for to look after/take care of somebody who is sick, very old, very young, etc.

, making and she made

weed (n) a wild plant growing where it is not wanted, especially among crops or garden plants

water (v) to pour water on plants, etc.

UNIT 1   Modern English Fairy Tales

Once she finished, she headed back into the little hut, but stopped when she noticed something shining in the moonlight. She bent down and picked up a little gold coin. With joy, she hurried back into the hut and showed it to her old husband and good daughter.

"Look! We have been blessed by the little folk! This coin is from the leprechaun, I'm sure!" declared the old woman, showing off the shining gold coin. Her husband, who was superstitious, looked at it carefully.

"Indeed, my wife. We have been blessed by the leprechauns. What have you given to them to gain this, though?"

He wondered out loud, unsure of the notion. But his wife was beside herself with joy.

---

head　　ⓥ　　to move in a particular direction
bless　　ⓥ　　to be provided with a particular cherished thing by a higher power like God
folk　　ⓝ　　people in general
leprechaun　ⓝ　(in Irish stories) a creature like a little man, with magic powers
declare　ⓥ　to state something firmly and clearly
, showing off　　and she showed off/ while she was showing off
show off　　to try to impress others by talking about your abilities, possessions, etc.
, who　　because he
, unsure (= , being unsure)　　because he was unsure
was (be) beside herself (oneself) with ~　　to be in a state of very great, uncontrolled emotion because of ~

"We shall eat on this for seven days and seven nights!" exclaimed the old woman. And in the morning, she went to the market and bought food for seven days and seven nights. For seven days and seven nights, the old man, his wife and their good daughter ate heartily and did not go hungry.

Once the food ran out, the couple began to fail in health once more, and the old woman carried on her care of her garden every morning and every evening.

One evening, perhaps a week later, the old woman looked up to the sky and said, "Oh how I wish I had a gold coin to feed my husband and my belly." And on her way back into the hut, she found something shimmering in her garden once again, and this time picked up two gold coins.

With great joy, the old wife showed the coins to her old husband, who was curious again.

"Oh look, husband mine! We have been blessed once more by the little folk! We shall eat two weeks on these two gold coins!"

---

shall (aux)		used with *I* and *we* for talking about or predicting the future; will
heartily (adv)		with obvious enjoyment and enthusiasm
go hungry		to miss a meal and end up hungry
once (conj)		as soon as; when
ran (run) out		to use up or finish a supply of something
carried (carry) on		to continue doing something
feed (v)		to give food to a person or an animal
belly (n)		the part of the body below the chest; stomach
shimmer (v)		to shine with a soft light that seems to move slightly
curious (a)		having a strong desire to know about something
husband mine		husband of mine; my husband

UNIT 1 Modern English Fairy Tales

And they did, eating heartily upon the food that the two gold coins had gotten for them. After the food had run out once more, and the health of the elderly couple and their good daughter began to fade once again, the elderly woman went out to tend to her garden every morning and every evening.

One evening, the old woman looked up again to the sky and declared, "Oh! If only I had some more gold coins to feed my husband and my belly, and to live in a bigger hut."

But there was no gold coin to be found on her way back to the hut.

Every evening, the old wife searched and waited for gold, but none was to be found. At last, on the seventh night of waiting, the old woman looked up to the sky and declared, "Oh! I would do and give anything for some gold coins! I don't have much, but I would give whatever I can."

The old wife finished tending to her little garden, and returned to the little hut.

---

elderly (a) quite old; past middle age
fade (v) to lose strength or vitality; wane
declare (v) to state something firmly and clearly
if only used to say that you wish something was true or that something had happened
none (pron) not one of a group of people or things; not any
was (be) to can
whatever (pron) anything or everything

But when she turned to head back, she stumbled upon a little wooded box. Curious, she opened the box, and discovered many gold coins. Excited and happy, the old wife returned to the little hut, and quickly showed her husband.

"Alas! The little folk have blessed us forevermore! Now we don't have to worry about being poor or hungry!"

But the old husband expressed concern.

"But my dear wife! What do we have to give the little folk for this? We are but very poor old folk with a little garden, a little hut, and a good daughter."

But the old woman did not heed the words of her old husband, and continued on her way with happiness.

---

turn   (v)   to move your body or part of your body so as to face or start moving in a different direction

head   (v)   to move in a particular direction

stumble   (v)   to hit your foot against something while you are walking or running and almost fall

Curious,   Being curious (= as she was curious)

Excited and happy,   (Being) excited and being happy (= As she was excited and happy)

alas   (int)   used to express sorrow, regret, grief, compassion, or apprehension
of danger or evil

forevermore   (adv)   forever /eternally

express   (v)   to show or make known a feeling, an opinion, etc. by words, looks or actions

concern   (n)   a feeling of worry, especially one that is shared by many people

but   (prep)   only

heed   (v)   to pay careful attention to somebody's advice or warning

35

Later that evening, the old woman awoke to the sound of screeching coming from her little garden, and she went outside to investigate.

"Is that you, one of the little folk of legend?"

She asked curiously, searching the garden. Among the larger flowers, a little man with a distorted face peeked out from behind, and startled the old woman.

"I do believe you owe me for my gold coins," declared the leprechaun, holding out his hand. The old woman worried a moment.

"But I have nothing to give you! We are nothing but poor folk with a little hut, a little garden and a good daughter."

But the leprechaun would not give up.

"Then I want your little garden and your good daughter in exchange for my coins."

---

screech ⓥ to make a loud high unpleasant sound

investigate ⓥ to carefully examine the facts of a situation, an event, a crime, etc. to find out the truth about it or how it happened

legend ⓝ a story from ancient times about people and events, that may or may not be true; this type of story

curiously (adv) in a way of having a strong desire to know about something

distorted ⓐ pulled or twisted out of shape

peek ⓥ to be just visible

startle ⓥ to surprise somebody suddenly in a way that slightly shocks or frightens them

do (aux) to emphasize what you are saying

owe ⓥ to feel that you ought to do something for somebody or give them something, especially because they have done something for you hold out

nothing but   only

The Gold Coin

But the old woman loved her daughter dearly, and could not find it in herself to give away her good daughter.

"I'm sorry, but I can not do that."

"Then I want my coins back."

"But I had fed my family on your coins!"

"Then I want the food you had bought with my gold coins," demanded the leprechaun.

"But we had eaten the food," declared the desperate old wife.

"Then I want one limb for every coin. I gave you one hundred coins, so I want one hundred limbs."

"But I don't have one hundred limbs to give!"

The old wife was now frightened. The leprechaun suddenly became angry.

---

dearly (adv)   very much
find it in herself (oneself) to ~   to have the courage or compassion to do something
give away   to give something as a gift
demand (v)   to ask for something very firmly
desperate (a)   feeling or showing that you have little hope and are ready to do anything without worrying about danger to yourself or others
limb (n)   an arm or a leg; a similar part of an animal, such as a wing

UNIT 1 Modern English Fairy Tales

"You have gone back on your word, old hag! You promised something in return for my coins, and I was kind enough to give them to you. You have gone back on your word and lied to me. You have become greedy in times of need, for you need not have taken the gold. So, you should pay for it."

And before the old woman could blink, the leprechaun was gone, leaving her in the darkness of her little garden.

The next morning, the old wife remained in bed, and when her old husband and good daughter came to rouse her, she refused.

"Oh my family! I have done wrong to the little folk! I have lied to the little folk! I should have been thankful!"

And her husband realized there was nothing he could do for her, and called for the good doctor.

---

gone (go) back on your (one's) word   to fail to keep a promise; to break a promise

hag (n)   an ugly and/or unpleasant old woman

greedy (a)   wanting more money, power, food, etc. than you really need

for (conj)   used to introduce the reason for something mentioned in the previous statement

blink (v)   when you blink or blink your eyes or your eyes blink, you shut and open your eyes quickly

leaving (leave) (v)   to go away from a place without taking something/somebody with you

rouse (v)   to wake somebody up, especially when they are sleeping deeply

call for   to require; demand

That night, a horrible storm came, flooding the river between the village and the forest.

Seven days and six nights passed, and at last the doctor was able to reach the little hut in the forest.

Tap. Tap. Tap.

He rapped on the door of the little hut, but there was no response.

Tap. Tap. Tap.

He rapped again and again with no response. Thus the good doctor let himself in, and came upon a wicked sight in the little hut.

At the tiny table in the little kitchen sat the old man, his wife and their good daughter. Their stomachs were sliced open, revealing their bowels to the floor.

The doctor approached, and something that shined caught his eye. There, on the table of the little kitchen in the little hut, existed a little gold coin.

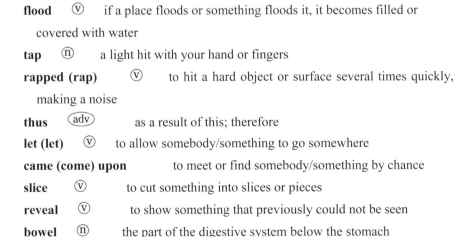

flood (v)   if a place floods or something floods it, it becomes filled or covered with water
tap (n)   a light hit with your hand or fingers
rapped (rap) (v)   to hit a hard object or surface several times quickly, making a noise
thus (adv)   as a result of this; therefore
let (let) (v)   to allow somebody/something to go somewhere
came (come) upon   to meet or find somebody/something by chance
slice (v)   to cut something into slices or pieces
reveal (v)   to show something that previously could not be seen
bowel (n)   the part of the digestive system below the stomach

UNIT 1 Modern English Fairy Tales

QUESTIONS   Answer the following questions in English.

1. Do you think that the old woman was selfish? What do you think so?

2. What kind of character is the leprechaun?

3. What do you think the lesson of this story is?

4. What are the three main parts in the story: introduction, body, and conclusion?

5. Would you have done anything different from the old woman? What is your reason?

The Gift

In a time long ago, but maybe not too long of a time, there was once a creature of a grotesque nature. He had the upper half of man and the lower half of a goat. Humans feared this creature when they looked upon it.

One day, or maybe night, a farmer of a little village was tending to his fields, when the grotesque creature startled him. He spotted it in his fields, holding one of his plows threateningly. Quickly, the farmer ran back to the comfort of his little farmhouse and little family.

---

once (adv)   at some time in the past

creature (n)   a living thing, real or imaginary, that can move around, such as an animal

grotesque (a)   extremely ugly in a strange way that is often frightening or amusing

nature (n)   real appearance, natural looks

tend to   to care for somebody/something

, when   and then

startle (v)   to surprise somebody suddenly in a way that slightly shocks or frightens them

spotted (spot) (v)   to see or notice a person or thing, especially suddenly or when it is not easy to do so

, holding   while he was holding/and he held

plow (n)   a large piece of farming equipment with one or several curved blades, pulled by a tractor or by animals

threateningly (adv)   in a way of expressing a threat of harm or violence

comfort (n)   the state of being physically relaxed and free from pain

UNIT 1   Modern English Fairy Tales

On another day, or perhaps night, a young woman was sewing her linens when she caught sight of the grotesque creature. It was holding something out to her, but she was afraid and ran back to her home, leaving the creature alone in the field.

Always, it happened this way, and the creature became a subject of terror among the little village.

On a rather cold day, a child was playing in the snowy woods, came across a branch, and broke his foot. Such an agony came across the child that he cried.

For an hour, maybe two, the little boy cried. When he felt he could cry no more, he noticed a rustling coming from behind him.

---

sew   ⓥ   to use a needle and thread to make stitches in cloth
linen   ⓝ   a type of cloth made from flax (= a plant with blue flowers), used to make high-quality clothes, sheets, etc.
catch sight of   find
hold out   to put your hand or arms, or something in your hand, towards somebody, especially to give or offer something
subject   ⓝ   a thing or person that is being discussed, described or dealt with
terror   ⓝ   a feeling of extreme fear
came (come) across   to meet or find somebody/something by chance
such ~ that ~   used to emphasize the great degree of something
agony   ⓝ   extreme physical or mental pain
notice   ⓥ   to see or hear somebody/something
rustling (rustle)   ⓥ   to make a soft, quiet crackling sound like that (= the sound) caused by the movement of dry leaves

He turned and saw a creature that bore the chest and head of man and the body of goat. The child quit his tears, and watched the creature curiously. The creature, in turn, watched with equal curiosity.

With no words, the creature pointed to the child's pained foot, and the child nodded. Without hesitation, the creature held out a leaf, which he placed onto the child's pain, instantly relieving it.

"You are not afraid of me, my boy?" asked the creature, and the child shook his head. The creature smiled and the two of them played together for hours, maybe days.

---

bore (bear) (v) to show something; to carry something so that it can be seen
chest (n) the top part of the front of the body, between the neck and the stomach
quit (quit) (v) to stop
curiously (adv) with a strong desire to know about something
in turn next/as well
curiosity (n) a strong desire to know about something
pained (a) hurt or troubled
nodded (nod) (v) to move your head up and down to show agreement, understanding, etc.
hesitation (n) to be slow to speak or act because you feel uncertain or nervous
, which and it
relieving (relieve) (v) to remove or reduce an unpleasant feeling or pain
shook his head (shake one's head) to turn your head from side to side as a way of saying 'no' or to show sadness, disapproval, doubt, etc.

UNIT 1　Modern English Fairy Tales

When the child told the creature that he must return home, the kind creature gave the child a wrapped gift, and told him to open it when he felt lonely. And the child thanked the creature and returned home.

It was not a long moment before the little boy became lonely, and he opened the wrapped gift from the kind creature. Inside, was a little wooden flute crafted from the finest wood with the finest finish. The little boy played the flute, and turned when he heard a voice.

"You have called to me, my boy. I am most happy to be in your company again."

And they became good friends. For a long time they played with each other, and the kind, grotesque creature always protected him. When the child became of old age and passed, the creature protected and played with his children and his grandchildren, and many generations passed.

---

wrapped (wrap)　(v)　to cover something completely in paper or other material, for example when you are giving it as a present

wooden　(a)　made of wood

crafted (craft)　(v)　to make something using special skills, especially with your hands

finest (fine)　(a)　of high quality; good

finish　(n)　the last covering of paint, polish, etc. that is put onto the surface of something

most happy　　very happy

company　(n)　the fact of being with somebody else and not alone

pass　(v)　to die

generation　(n)　the average time in which children grow up, become adults and have children of their own, (usually considered to be about 30 years)

The Gift

QUESTIONS   Answer the following questions in English.

1. Why were the people afraid of the creature?

2. Why wasn't the boy scared of the creature?

3. What is "The Gift"?

4. How did the relationship between the creature and the boy proceed?

5. Which do you prefer: a person with an attractive appearance, but a bad character, or a person with an unattractive appearance, but a good character? Why is your reason?

UNIT 1   Modern English Fairy Tales

The Fox and the Rabbit

Somewhere, in a forbidden land far away, there lived many animals of many different kinds. Mostly, they lived in peaceful harmony, and followed all the rules set by the great grandfather Eagle who oversaw all the happenings on Mother Earth.

Although there was great peace among all kin in the forest, there was a trickster who enjoyed causing havoc among his friends. Sometimes, he would come from his dwelling in the ground and steal from the other animals, or he would cause suspicion among the groups with his clever words of treachery.

---

forbidden (forbid) ⓥ   to command (a person) not to do or have something or not to enter some place

the Eagle   The Eagle or Aquila is part of the Summer Triangle. It has long been known by many cultures.

oversaw (oversee) ⓥ   to watch somebody/something and make sure that a job or an activity is done correctly

kin ⓝ   a person's relatives or family

trickster ⓝ   a person who tricks or cheats people

causing (cause) ⓥ   to make something happen, especially something bad or unpleasant

havoc ⓝ   a situation in which there is a lot of damage, destruction or confusion

dwelling ⓝ   a house, flat/apartment, etc. where a person lives

suspicion ⓝ   a feeling that somebody has done something wrong, illegal or dishonest, even though you have no proof

treachery ⓝ   behavior that involves not being loyal to somebody who trusts you

The Fox and the Rabbit

One day, on a beautiful and sunny day, Rabbit decided to visit the watering hole. It was beautiful but hot, and Rabbit wanted to enjoy the day in full, with a nice big gulp of fresh spring water. She spent her time traveling, stopping to sniff flowers and to gaze at the large, white puffy clouds that littered Father Sky.

At last, she reached the watering hole, and happily began drinking the fresh, cool water. There was a sudden noise in the bush behind her, and Rabbit stood up to be sure that it was not a predator who would be interested in devouring her. But alas, it was just Fox who popped up from the bush, and he courteously made a bow before her.

---

watering (water) ⓥ to pour water on plants, etc.
in full in total, without exception, in its entirety
gulp ⓝ a large and hurried swallow
sniff ⓥ to smell (with pleasure), as in investigating
gaze ⓥ to look steadily and intently, as with great interest or wonder
puffy ⓐ looking soft, round and white
litter ⓥ to be spread around a place, making it look untidy
bush ⓝ a large uncleared area covered with mixed plant growth, as a jungle
predator ⓝ an animal that kills and eats other animals
devour ⓥ to eat all of something quickly, especially because you are very hungry
alas ⓘⁿᵗ used to show you are sad or sorry
courteously ⓐᵈᵛ in a polite manner, especially in a way that shows respect
made (make) a bow to move your head or the top half of your body forwards and downwards as a sign of respect or to say hello or goodbye

47

UNIT 1 Modern English Fairy Tales

"Please! Do not be afraid of me, Rabbit! It is just I, Fox!"

Rabbit's eyes narrowed with suspicion. She turned away and began to drink the water again. Fox sighed, coming to stand next to her.

"Oh, Rabbit! Has something turned you against me? Are we not friends, my sister?"

Rabbit stopped drinking and turned to Fox.

"Fox, I do not understand what you want, but you are up to no good! I will not allow a single white fur on my back to be ruined by your trickery today!"

Fox tilted his head back and laughed.

"Oh, Rabbit! Do not fear! Today I am merely offering you something good! I do not do this normally, but I would like to show you something interesting!"

---

turn away   to move your body or part of your body so as to face or start moving in a different direction

, coming   and he came

turn ~ against   to stop or make somebody stop being friendly towards somebody

up to no good   doing something bad

fur (n)   the soft thick mass of hair that grows on the body of some animals

ruined (ruin) (v)   to damage something so badly that it loses all its value, pleasure, etc; to spoil something

trickery (n)   the use of tricks to deceive someone

tilt (v)   to incline or bend from a vertical (= straight up and down) position

merely (adv)   used meaning 'only' or 'simply' to emphasize a fact or something that you are saying

Curiosity got the better of Rabbit, and she reluctantly followed him. It was possible that Fox could be true to his word today. They walked for a time, and Fox took Rabbit deep, deep into the forest; when at last Crow cawed from above, coming down to the floor in front of them.

"Caw! What is it that brings you, young Rabbit, to the dark place of the forest? Caw!"

Rabbit gestured towards Fox.

"It is Fox who brought me here. He said he had something to show to me!"

Crow laughed.

"Caw! You should turn back now! Caw! Fox is lying to you! Caw!" warned Crow.

---

got (get) the better of ~ win a victory over ~

reluctantly (adv) hesitatingly before doing something because you do not want to do it or because you are not sure that it is the right thing to do

; when and then

crow (n) a large bird, completely or mostly black, with a rough unpleasant cry

caw (v) utter a cry, characteristic of crows

, coming down and it came down

caw (n) the loud, unpleasant sound that is made by birds such as crows

turn back to return the way you have come; to make somebody/something do this

lying (lie) (v) to say or write something that you know is not true

warn (v) to tell somebody about something, especially something dangerous or unpleasant that is likely to happen, so that they can avoid it

UNIT 1   Modern English Fairy Tales

But Rabbit shook her head, her floppy ears flopping on her head.

"This can not be true! Fox gave his word to me!"

"You are unwise to listen to the word of Fox! Caw! Go back!"

Crow's warning sounded ominous to Rabbit, but she did not take heed of his words.

"I am sorry, Crow! Please return to Father Sky and leave me be! Fox is my friend and has given me his word!"

Together, Fox and Rabbit continued forward, leaving Crow behind. They walked more and more, and eventually Rabbit's little feet began to hurt her. But they still walked on, and Fox would not pause to rest.

---

shook her head (shake one's head)   to turn your head from side to side as a way of saying 'no' or to show sadness, disapproval, doubt, etc.

, her floppy ears flopping   and her floppy ears flopped

floppy   ⓐ   hanging or falling loosely; not hard and stiff

flopping (flop)   ⓥ   to fall, move or hang in a heavy or awkward way, without control

gave his word (give one's word)   give a promise or guarantee that you will do something or that something will happen or is true

ominous   ⓐ   suggesting that something bad is going to happen in the future

take heed of ~   to pay careful attention to somebody/something

leave me be (leave one be)   to accept a situation, allowing it to be the same and to leave the person alone

word   ⓝ   a promise or guarantee that you will do something or that something will happen or is true

, leaving   and they (= Fox and Rabbit) left

eventually   ⓐdv   at the end of a period of time or a series of events

pause   ⓥ   to stop talking or doing something for a short time before continuing

The Fox and the Rabbit

"Fox! Where is it we are going? My feet hurt and I am afraid I can not go any farther!"

Rabbit wailed, plopping down onto the ground with exhaustion. Fox approached her.

"You are sure you can not go farther?"

"Yes," replied Rabbit.

"You can not move any more?"

"No," replied Rabbit.

And with that response, Fox laughed and began to circle the exhausted rabbit.

"Well then! It is time for me to gobble you up!"

He pounced, but Rabbit hopped away sluggishly. She was quite tired.

"Fox! What are you doing? You gave your word. You would not trick me!"

---

wail (v) to make a long loud high cry because you are sad or in pain

plopping (plop) (v) to sit or lie down heavily or in a relaxed way

exhaustion (n) the state of being very tired

exhausted (a) very tired

gobble ~ (up) (v) to eat something very fast, in a way that people consider rude or greedy

pounce (v) to move suddenly forwards in order to attack or catch somebody/something

sluggishly (adv) in a slow manner to perform or respond to stimulation

would (aux) used in place of *will*, to make a statement or form a question less direct or blunt (= to the point)

trick (v) to make somebody believe something which is not true, especially in order to cheat them

UNIT 1 Modern English Fairy Tales

Fox laughed.

"But I have not lied! I said that I had to show you something, and I do! I will show you the inside of my hungry belly!"

And like that, Rabbit was gobbled up by Fox.

The next day, another rabbit appeared at the watering hole, and Fox lured her into the forest, and Crow again warned the rabbit, who did not listen, and Fox gobbled her up.

This happened for three days, until the rabbits began to notice the decline in their numbers. They consulted with Black Rabbit, who was the head of all the rabbits in the forest. Black Rabbit decided to figure out what was going on.

On the fourth day, his investigation brought him to the watering hole, where Fox was waiting for his next prey.

---

belly (n)   the part of the body below the chest

lure (v)   to persuade or trick somebody to go somewhere or to do something by promising them a reward

, who   but he

, until   and at last

decline (n)   a continuous decrease in the number, value, quality, etc. of something

, who   and he

investigation (n)   a careful examination or search in order to discover facts or gain information.

, where   and there

prey (n)   an animal hunted or caught by another for food

The Fox and the Rabbit

Black Rabbit addressed him suspiciously, "Fox, what are you doing here?" Fox replied innocently, "Come with me. I have something interesting to show you."

Against his better judgement, Black Rabbit followed Fox away from the watering hole. Fox and Black Rabbit were stopped by Crow, who cawed out, "It is not wise to listen to Fox!"

This time, Black Rabbit acknowledged Crow, "I take heed to your words. Please feel free to accompany us."

Fox spluttered with a protest, "But this is for your eyes alone, Black Rabbit! I do not want to share our secret!"

But Black Rabbit shook his head.

"Fox, if you are true to your word, then you will have no problems showing me with an audience! There should be no secrets kept from Mother Earth, and we are all part of Mother Earth."

---

address (v)   to speak to

suspiciously (adv)   in a way that shows you think somebody has done something wrong

innocently (adv)   in a way of having little experience of the world.

acknowledge (v)   to accept that somebody/something has a particular authority or status

accompany (v)   to travel or go somewhere with somebody

splutter (v)   to speak quickly and with difficulty, making soft spitting sounds, because you are angry or embarrassed

protest (n)   the expression of strong disagreement with or opposition to something; a statement or an action that shows this

are (be) true to your (one's) word   do what one promises to do

UNIT 1   Modern English Fairy Tales

With this, Fox could not argue, and he begrudgingly allowed Crow to come along.

When Black Rabbit began to tire, he turned to Crow.

"Oh Crow!" he exclaimed.

"My feet are beginning to tire, and it is thus to be a long journey home! Please carry me on your back!"

And Crow nodded in spite of the appalled look on Fox's face, allowing the small rabbit to ride between his wings.

---

argue (v)   to speak angrily to somebody because you disagree with them
begrudgingly (adv)   given or done unwillingly
tire (v)   to become tired and feel as if you want to sleep or rest; to make somebody feel this way
turn (v)   to move your body or part of your body so as to face or start moving in a different direction
exclaim (v)   to cry out or speak suddenly or excitedly, as from surprise, delight, horror, etc.
thus (adv)   as a result of something just mentioned
nod (v)   to move your head up and down to show agreement, understanding, etc.
in spite of ~   not stopped by ~; regardless of ~
appalled (a)   feeling or showing horror or disgust at something unpleasant or wrong
, allowing   and he allowed
allow (v)   to let somebody/something do something; to let something happen or be done

The Fox and the Rabbit

When they finally arrived at the destination, Crow set Black Rabbit down. Fox angrily began to circle around them.

"Now! I am hungry and must eat! Black Rabbit! You will feed me now!"

Despite Fox's anger, Black Rabbit remained calm.

"But Fox, my brother, you said that you had something to show me?"

"I do! The inside of my belly!"

Fox lunged at Black Rabbit, but Black Rabbit was not tired, so he hopped quickly out of the way.

"Fox! There is no use! You have not tired me enough to catch me! I can still run quickly!"

Black Rabbit turned, running quickly on all fours back towards the watering hole. Crow cawed loudly from Father Sky.

Arriving at the watering hole, Black Rabbit waited for Fox.

---

destination (n)   a place to which somebody/something is going or being sent

feed (v)   to give food to a person or an animal

despite (prep)   used to show that something happened or is true although something else might have happened to prevent it

calm (a)   not excited, nervous or upset

lunge (v)   to make a sudden powerful forward movement, especially in order to attack somebody or take hold of something

there is no use   it is useless

on all fours   bent over with hands and knees on the ground

Arriving ~,   When he arrived ~,

UNIT 1 Modern English Fairy Tales

Fox arrived shortly, huffing and puffing.

"Black Rabbit! Surrender! I am hungry!" called Fox.

"You may not eat me this day! I am nothing but a black rabbit, not filling enough to satisfy the hunger of a tricky fox!"

"You will do for now! And then, I will eat another rabbit tomorrow!"

Black Rabbit was much too wise for Fox.

"Why do you eat a small meal every day when you can eat a larger meal once a week?"

Suddenly, Fox was confused.

"But that is not possible!"

Black Rabbit shook his head.

"It is! If you go behind that tree there, you will find a nice, large meal that will satisfy you for an entire week!"

---

shortly　(adv)　　soon

, huffing and puffing　　while he was huffing and puffing

huffing and puffing (huff and puff)　　to breathe in a noisy way because of great fatigue or tiredness

surrender　(v)　　to admit that you have been defeated and want to stop fighting; to allow yourself to be caught, taken prisoner, etc.

nothing but　　only; no more than

filling　(a)　　making your stomach feel full

tricky　(a)　　marked by skill in deception/clever but likely to trick you

will do　　be good enough or available

entire　(a)　　(used when you are emphasizing that the whole of something is involved) including everything, everyone or every part

The Fox and the Rabbit

Excited a lot, Fox immediately ran behind the tree, finding not a meal but angry Brother Bear. Fox screamed, running away from the watering hole and back into the forest.

Black Rabbit approached angry Brother Bear.

"Brother, I must thank you for your kindness in helping us poor rabbits."

Brother Bear shook his head with a gruffness.

"Fox has caused great trouble within the forest, and should be punished as such. Fox should not return here anymore."

With that being said, all of the rabbits of the forest's watering hole rejoiced, happy to be without that trickster Fox.

Excited ~ ,	Because he was excited ~ ,
, finding	but he found
but (prep)	except; apart from
gruffness (n)	an abrupt, discourteous, unfriendly, and impatient manner
rejoice (v)	to express great happiness about something

57

UNIT 1 Modern English Fairy Tales

QUESTIONS   Answer the following questions in English.

1. Why did Rabbit follow Fox?

2. What should Rabbit have done to avoid being devoured by Fox?

3. Why didn't Black Rabbit become tired like the other rabbits?

4. How did Black Rabbit outsmart Fox?

5. What made Fox run away from the watering hole?

Trees

A long time ago, there existed a large, uncultivated forest about thirty miles west of the Imperial Forbidden City.

A white rabbit hopped along an old beaten path. He sprung along, changing his direction swiftly as if he knew where he was headed. On his way, the white rabbit leapt over a hill, past a hollow log which marked an entrance of sorts, ornamented in writhing vines and thorns.

---

uncultivated ⓐ not used for growing crops
Imperial ⓐ connected with an empire
forbidden ⓐ not allowed; prohibited (forbid: not to allow, to prohibit)
hopped (hop) ⓥ to move by jumping with all or two feet together
beaten ⓐ much traveled by walking somewhere or by pressing branches down and walking over them
sprung (spring) ⓥ to move suddenly and with one quick movement in a particular direction
, changing and he changed
as if in a way that suggests something
was (be) headed to move in a particular direction towards a destination
leapt (leap) ⓥ to jump high or a long way
hollow ⓐ having a hole or empty space inside
log ⓝ a thick piece of wood that is cut from a tree
of sorts of a mediocre/second-rate or inferior kind
ornament ⓥ to add decoration to something
writhing (writhe) ⓥ to be intertwined with or to be twisted together
vine ⓝ a climbing plant
thorn ⓝ a small sharp pointed part on the stem of some plants, such as roses

UNIT 1　Modern English Fairy Tales

The forest had been thriving with life since the dawn of civilization. It stood strong and alive, amidst the moonlit shadows and living things that dwelled within.

The little white rabbit came to a sudden halt and sat himself upon a tree stump. The white rabbit lifted his chin upwards and stared blankly off into the expanse of sky above him while paying no mind to the greenery which had surrounded him for some time.

---

thriving (thrive)　ⓥ　to become, and continue to be, successful, strong, healthy, etc.

dawn　ⓝ　the beginning or first signs of something

civilization　ⓝ　a state of human society that is very developed and organized

amidst　prep　in the middle of or during something, especially something that causes excitement or fear

moonlit　ⓐ　lit by the moon　(light-lit-lit)

dwell　ⓥ　to live somewhere

halt　ⓝ　an act of stopping the movement or progress of somebody/something

stump　ⓝ　the bottom part of a tree left in the ground after the rest has fallen or been cut down

chin　ⓝ　the part of the face below the mouth and above the neck

stare　ⓥ　to look at somebody/something for a long time, especially in a way that is unfriendly or that shows surprise

blankly　adv　in a way of showing no feeling, understanding or interest

expanse　ⓝ　a wide and open area of something, especially land or water

greenery　ⓝ　attractive green leaves and plants

Trees

This is where the tree brothers had loomed for centuries, over the lush vegetation and animals of the forest. Their branches extended far, wide, long and high. They extended higher than any other living thing in the forest. Their life stretched far beyond those around them and was far-reaching in stature. Their roots were deeply embedded in the rich soil of Amazonia, in the forest where animals and insects scurried about.

---

loom (v) to appear as a large shape that is not clear, especially in a frightening or threatening way
lush (a) growing thickly and strongly in a way that is attractive; covered in healthy grass and plants
vegetation (n) plants in general, especially the plants that are found in a particular area or environment
extend (v) to cover a particular area, distance or length of time
stretch (v) to spread over an area of land
far-reaching (a) having a wide range, influence, or effect
stature (n) importance or reputation gained by achievement or ability
embedded (embed) (v) to fix or become fixed firmly and deeply in a surrounding solid mass
soil (n) the top layer of the earth in which plants, trees, etc. grow
insect (n) any small creature with six legs and a body divided into three parts. Insects usually also have wings
scurried (scurry) (v) to run with quick short steps
about (adv) in many directions; here and there

The three tree brothers survived several seasons of disaster. From the Barbarians of the North, the youngest survived a fire, which had set his branches ablaze. He was filled with hope when he had felt the strong winds extinguish the hurtful flames.

The middle brother feared the wind that blew so furiously from the south, for deforestation had cleared up what was once an incredibly dense rain forest. Though the feeling of protection was quickly deteriorating, his bark had matured in its old age and grew resilient and strong.

---

disaster (n) an unexpected event, such as a very bad accident, a flood or a fire, that kills a lot of people or causes a lot of damage

barbarian (n) a member of a primitive or uncivilized people

ablaze (adv) burning quickly and strongly

extinguish (v) to make a fire stop burning or a light stop shining

hurtful (a) making you feel upset and offended

flame (n) a hot bright stream of burning gas that comes from something that is on fire

furiously (adv) in a wild and stormy manner

for (conj) because, since

deforestation (n) the act of cutting down or burning the trees in an area

what (pron) the thing or things that

dense (a) containing a lot of people, things, plants, etc. with little space between them

deteriorating (deteriorate) (v) to become worse

bark (n) the outer covering of a tree

mature (v) to become fully grown or developed

resilient (a) able to feel better quickly after something unpleasant such as shock, injury, etc.

The winds had evaporated what little water was retained, but the middle brother persevered.

The eldest outlasted countless fires, wind storms, and dry spells with patience and perseverance as he stood there rooted in the ground. Together the three tree brothers stayed strong.

Although their exteriors were ravaged by all the tyranny, nature's efforts were rendered powerless against their deeply intertwined and tightly wound roots.

---

evaporate (v)   to convert or change into a vapor (= a mass of very small drops of liquid in the air, for example steam)

retain (v)   to continue to hold or contain something

persevere (v)   to continue trying to do or achieve something despite difficulties

outlast (v)   to continue to exist or take part in an activity for a longer time than somebody/something

countless (a)   very many; too many to be counted or mentioned

spell (n)   a short period of time during which something lasts

perseverance (n)   the quality of continuing to try to achieve a particular aim despite difficulties

exterior (n)   the outside of something, especially a building

ravage (v)   to damage something badly

tyranny (n)   unfair or cruel use of power or authority

render (v)   to cause somebody/something to be in a particular state or condition

intertwine (v)   to join or become joined by twisting or twining together

wound (wind) (v)   to wrap or twist something around itself or something else

UNIT 1 Modern English Fairy Tales

The tree brothers were fortified and strengthened from beneath. Together with all the trees, flowers and plants, which were rooted near them, they stood together. Their unadulterated roots intertwined close together were all that they needed to outlast natural forces.

---

fortified (fortify) ⓥ   to make somebody/yourself feel stronger, braver, etc.
strengthen ⓥ   to become stronger; to make somebody/something stronger
beneath   (adv)   under
unadulterated ⓐ   pure, or not mixed with anything else
outlast ⓥ   to live longer than

QUESTIONS   Answer the following questions in English.

1. How is the white rabbit involved in the story?

2. What trials has each of the three tree brothers faced?

3. Describe each of the three tree brothers' characteristics.

4. What gives the three tree brothers their strength?

5. What do the three tree brothers do for the forest?

UNIT 1 Modern English Fairy Tales

From the Future

This is the story of a far away land. A spaceship is floating in the dark, lonely universe. As you can never know if it was the egg or the chicken that came first, you can never tell what time it is. She is the ancestor or descendant of a human. She is tall and beautiful, with extremely red lips, sharp blue eyes, and short dark hair, wearing a violet loose garment.

She is talking into a recorder. The following are the contents of her audio recording:

---

floating (float) ⓥ   to be suspended in or move through space as if supported by a liquid

ancestor ⓝ   a person who was a member of one's family a long time ago and from whom one is descended

descendant ⓝ   a person considered as descended from some ancestor or race

loose ⓐ   free to move around without control

garment ⓝ   a piece of clothing

content ⓝ   the things that are contained or involved in something

audio ⓐ   connected with sound that is recorded

From the Future

Have you ever had the feeling that you were being followed by something or some idea? This is subconsciousness, or metapsychology, which has been passed on to us by our ancestors, who will turn out to be our descendants as well. You are in the process of making this subconciousness come true if you are truly aware of facing reality.

Fairies are on both sides, good and bad. The former is the gods' group, and the latter is the devils' group. Both groups are made up of our descendants, who have gained three superpowers: space-control, birth-control, and time-control. All descendants have the ability to fly, live eternally, and time travel. As is often the case with a power struggle, the group in control tries to maintain peace, while the opposition aims for destruction. Once control has been obtained, dominance

subconsciousness	(n)	the part of the mind below the level of conscious perception
metapsychology	(n)	speculative thought dealing with concepts extending beyond the limits of psychology as an empirical science
passed (pass) on		to give or to transfer possession of
the former		the first of two things or people mentioned
the latter		the second of two things or people mentioned
struggle	(n)	an energetic attempt to achieve something
maintain	(v)	to keep up or carry on; continue
opposition	(n)	the action of opposing, resisting, or combating
aim	(v)	to plan, intend or have something as one's purpose or goal
destruction	(n)	the termination of something by causing so much damage to it that it can not be repaired or no longer exists
once	(conj)	as soon as; if ever; when
dominance	(n)	the state that exists when one person or group has power over another

will last almost eternally in the future.

We, humans, have experienced three big stages during our existence. The first, a long time ago, around 250 million to 66 million years ago, was the dinosaur age in which every animal grew huge due to radioactivity. The second was the time when Jesus Christ, the messenger of the gods' group, was sent to the Earth in order to warn humans to maintain peace. The third was World War III, when the Earth was destroyed into a lifeless planet. This is why we are floating in outer space, trying to avoid this tragedy by going back in time and searching for a solution. In every stage, the battle between the gods' group and the devils' group has been taking place behind the scenes.

We, humans, have been trying to become the ultimate power, like the sun. My life is coming to an end, so I have taken it upon myself to record the truth, in order that you may understand our intentions and fulfill our goals.

---

last ⓥ to continue to exist or to function well
existence ⓝ the fact or state of existing or of being actual
dinosaur ⓝ any of several types of extinct giant reptiles
radioactivity ⓝ the spontaneous emission of a stream of particles or electromagnetic rays in nuclear decay
avoid ⓥ to prevent from happening
tragedy ⓝ an event resulting in great loss and misfortune
solution ⓝ an answer to a problem
taking (take) place happen
ultimate ⓐ of the greatest possible size or significance
taken (take) it upon myself (oneself) to ~ to accept responsibility for something without being asked to

The Secret of the Universe

The universe, the whole of creation, is kept in existence based on one great goal. It is beyond the existence, visible or invisible, or real or unreal. This means that "the universe is trying to accumulate a greater energy." In order to do so, the universe is active with a radiating energy and glow. This is the true form of the present world. Humans are no exception.

Humans are the only existing entity that can have a conscious mind and be aware of its actions. In that sense, humans are a superior entity to even the sun, which contains a far greater energy than humans. Humans are "struggling to obtain souls" as their final goal. Souls tend to live in close proximity to each other, whether consciously or unconsciously. The bigger a group the souls belong to, the greater advantages they will gain. The groups deal with souls, and ultimately they lead to the formation of religious ones. The religious groups are divided into Christians and non-Christians in the end. Islam falls into the Christian group in the long run. Buddhism only acts to narrate the process of the conflicts and others.

---

accumulate	(v)	to gather or collect, often in gradual degrees
radiating (radiate)	(v)	to send out rays or waves
glow	(n)	light emitted by a substance or object at a high temperature
sense	(n)	a meaning that is conveyed, as in speech or writing
entity	(n)	something that has a real existence; thing
struggling (struggle)	(v)	to make great efforts or try hard
proximity	(n)	nearness in place, time, relation, etc.
formation	(n)	the act of forming or establishing something
narrate	(v)	to tell a story
conflict	(n)	a struggle or clash between opposing forces; battle

UNIT 1   Modern English Fairy Tales

This process is similar to the one where elements gather into the formation of a fixed star, the sun, and die. In order for the sun to keep shining, it needs a supply of energy.

Humans only exist to fulfill their desires, which brings about a struggle to get various things accordingly. To gain energy and satisfaction through the struggle is the final purpose of human existence. This final struggle leads to "the struggle to obtain souls", because to obtain souls means to have them eternally. In the end, The purpose of human existence is a scramble to get souls, which is its final desire and goal. In Christianity, this scramble is expressed as "love," and people are promised eternal happiness, even if it does not exist in life, it will after death. In Buddhism, the process of the scramble is expressed as "the law of connection," or "causality — every effect has its cause." Here, the emphasis is placed on a calm state of mind, in which we should accept and be satisfied with things as they are, whether they are good or bad. This scramble for gaining souls is constantly and repeatedly performed in life, whether you are conscious of it or not, and even into death.

---

fixed star   an extremely distant star whose position appears not to move over a long period of time
supply   (n)   an amount of something available for use
brings (bring) about   to cause to happen, occur, or exist
accordingly   (adv)   as a result; therefore
scramble   (n)   a struggle for possession or gain
emphasis   (n)   special importance or significance
calm   (a)   free from excitement or passion; tranquil

Every human belongs to various groups, and tends to open up their minds to a certain degree within each group. From a higher perspective of the scramble to obtain souls, the true intentions of others can clearly be identified. You may feel a sensation of fear, as if you were alone in the darkness in the middle of the scramble, or you may be assailed by a feeling of solitude. It is in solitude that your existence or your value can not be noticed by anyone. The fact that the people around you can not notice or understand your feelings and ideas means that you do not exist on the Earth, as they become inanimate objects in your eyes then.

In this state of scrambling to gain souls, the people around you will urge you to join their own group through various means and methods, or attack you

---

degree (n) amount or extent

perspective (n) a way of regarding situations, facts, etc, and judging their relative importance

identified (identify) (v) to prove or recognize as being a certain person or thing

sensation (n) a feeling

assail (v) to attack someone physically or emotionally

solitude (n) the quality or state of being alone

value (n) worth, importance or usefulness

inanimate (a) not living

object (n) a thing that can be seen or felt

urge (v) to try to persuade or request earnestly (someone to do something)

means (n) the medium, method, or instrument used to obtain a result or achieve an end

method (n) a way of proceeding or doing something

UNIT 1 Modern English Fairy Tales

repeatedly if they judge that you may do them harm. This strong invitation, similar to a child innocently interfering with adults, will keep recurring throughout your life. However, when you think about how many advantages and disadvantages you will acquire by joining, you can not easily accept the invitation. Once you do accept, it will lead to a total loss of yourself; you may fearfully fall into apathy and irritability when thinking about the loss of your goals in life. Because of the feeling of solitude and eternal battle whether you are alive or dead, which will keep working on bare, defenseless souls, some may be afraid of this hard reality and become deranged. Others may return to a state of chaos. Still others, like Gautama Siddhartha, the founder of Buddhism, may gather people in an attempt to share this feeling by temporarily making them

---

innocently	adv	in an unexperienced or unworldly way
interfering (interfere)	v	to prevent, stop or slow down the progress of
recurring (recur)	v	to happen again or repeatedly
acquire	v	to get or gain
fearfully	adv	in fear
apathy	n	lack of emotion or interest
irritability	n	a characteristic tendency to show uncontrolled anger
bare	a	not wearing any clothes
deranged	a	mad, crazy, or insane
chaos	n	a condition or state of great disorder or confusion
founder	n	a person who establishes an institution, company, society, etc.
attempt	n	an effort made to accomplish something
temporarily	adv	for a limited time only; not permanently

understand this condition and may escape from the sense of solitude and fear. The invitation will linger relentlessly until you have responded favorably.

There is and will be no change at all to yourself after you have discovered this truth. Instead, you will just continue waiting for the time to come when your physique will crumble and perish, ignoring reality. That is to say, life is a process of being urged to make the decision whether or not to convert to one major group, Christianity. If you decline the offer, the group, regarding you as an enemy, will become a fiend that attacks you, trying to eliminate you.

---

escape (v) to get away from an unpleasant or dangerous situation
linger (v) to stay in a place or be slow in leaving it, often out of reluctance
relentlessly (adv) in a way that continues without becoming weaker
respond (v) to make a reply; answer
physique (n) bodily structure, proportions, appearance, and development shape, muscular development, etc.
crumble (v) to break down completely; to stop functioning
perish (v) to die or be destroyed, especially in a violent or untimely manner
ignoring (ignore) (v) to refuse to pay attention to; disregard
that is to say in other words; as follows
convert (v) to change one's religious faith or their belief
, regarding as they regard
regarding (regard) (v) to think of or consider in a specified way
fiend (n) a wicked or cruel person

UNIT 1 Modern English Fairy Tales

An individual human energy is interminable, therefore attractive to them. And yet it only exists in a finite amount. As you know, the energy of Christianity is immeasurable, and no match for any individual energy. Humans tend to gather in a shining place where a lot of energy exists in order to gain some of it. However, when you join Christianity, your soul disappears and is assimilated into the Christian soul, which means the eternal death of your soul.

It is natural to join Christianity if the bright light comes from it, but it is also natural to stick to your own light so that your energy will not be taken. Therefore, it is difficult to judge whether you are gaining or losing energy. As Christianity aims to become the sun as its ultimate goal, "the whole of creation, including humans, is the ancestor of the sun, holding a great ambition to be the sun someday." The sexual appetite functions to take in a great amount of energy, and through the fusion of two different multiplied energies, a new energy unit will be born. Even this unit looks similar to your own, it is a unique existence that starts working on its own activities. The appetite for food functions to

---

interminable	ⓐ	being or seeming to be without an end; endless
immeasurable	ⓐ	impossible to measure; limitless
no match for ~		be powerless against ~ ; not be somebody's equal ~
assimilate	ⓥ	to be or become absorbed
creation	ⓝ	the world and all things in it
appetite	ⓝ	an instinctive physical desire, especially one for food or drink
function	ⓥ	to operate or perform as specified; work properly
fusion	ⓝ	the state of being combined into one body
multiplied (multiply)	ⓥ	to increase or cause to increase in number, quantity, or degree

resupply energy through material consumption, and so does the appetite for sleep through the consumption of the floating energy in the air. Humans keep trying to expand their own energy while working on their own activities. Worry and joy are the result of failing and succeeding in energy resupply respectively. Children are only full of energy as a result of little use of their own energy. A human is born when they start to beat their own heart. A human dies not because their heartbeat stops of its own accord, but because it is stopped by their own will. The structure of a human body never changes from before life to after death. After all, all things being performed are the outcome of how the souls' energies are working.

    This is the end of recording.

---

resupply	(v)	to provide or make available again
material	(a)	formed or consisting of matter; physical
consumption	(n)	the act of using energy, food, or materials
expand	(v)	make bigger or wider in size, volume, or quantity
respectively	(adv)	in the same order as the people or things already mentioned
of its (one's) own accord		without being asked; of one's own free will
will	(n)	wish or desire
structure	(n)	the way in which something is arranged or organized
outcome	(n)	an end result; a consequence

UNIT 1 Modern English Fairy Tales

She finishes the recording and feels as calm as she can ever be.

There is no complete human existing at this time in the world. As she always does, she removes the mask from her face, revealing a dark silver machine with vertical and horizontal striping.

---

complete   ⓐ   including all the parts, etc. that are necessary; whole
remove   ⓥ   to take off (a piece of clothing)
, revealing   and she reveals
revealing (reveal)   ⓥ   to show; to allow to be seen
vertical   ⓐ   standing straight up at right angles to the earth's surface, or to a horizontal plane or line; upright
horizontal   ⓐ   at right angles to the vertical; parallel to level ground
striping   ⓝ   a pattern of stripes

QUESTIONS   Answer the following questions in English.

1. What kind of being is "she" in the story?

2. What are "fairies" mentioned as in the story?

3. What is the relationship between gods and devils in the story?

4. What is the final goal for humans in the story?

5. What should humans do to survive in the story?

UNIT 2
GRAMMAR

Part 1
Understanding Prepositions
―前置詞の理解―

UNIT 2　GRAMMAR

Ⅰ．前置詞とは？

　　前置詞は冠詞を伴った（ない場合や、代名詞の所有格がくる場合がある）名詞が後に続くのが、本来の形であるが、冠詞や名詞を伴わず単独で「副詞」として用いられたり、「形容詞」として使用される場合もある。ここでは前置詞としての使用方法を中心に、個々の前置詞の持っている意味を探ることにする。

Ⅱ．前置詞 "at" と "in" のイメージの違い

1．イメージの違い

at：「一地点」のイメージ
in：「入れ物の中」のイメージ

2．時間を表わす時

at： 時の流れの「1地点」
　　at the end of the day　（1日が終わる1地点→1日の終わりに）
in： 幅のある時間や空間の「入れ物の中に」
　　In the end, he accepted it.　（結局、彼はそれを受け入れた：一定の時間の最後に→最後に）

3．場所を表わす時

at：Meet me at the station.　（「駅で会いましょう。」駅という1地点で会う。駅のどこでも良いというイメージなので実際には会えないかも知れない）

82

in : Meet me in the station. (「駅の中で会いましょう」この方が範囲は絞られるが、まだ範囲が広いので合うのは難しいかもしれない) Meet me under the clock. (時計の下で会いましょう)などと限定した方が良い。

Ⅲ. 前置詞 "until (till)" と "by" のイメージ

1. 時間を表す時

① "until" の例

Stay until tomorrow afternoon.

(明日の午後までずっと滞在してください)

この until は継続する動作 stay「滞在する」が「終わるまで」の状況を表します。つまり、「明日の午後までは滞在してください」という意味です。until の前には stay「滞在する」や wait「待つ」のような、継続性の意味のある動詞が使われます。

Stay home until 6 : 00. (6時までずっと家にいてください)

② "by" の例

I'll leave by tomorrow afternoon.

(明日の午後までに出発します)

by は基準となる一地点「〜のそば」を表す前置詞です。例文では by が「〜までに」という期限を表します。until とはちがって、「終点までの一地点で動作が完了する」という意味です。by の前には leave や get のような「動作が完成する」という意味合いの動詞がきます。

Get home by 3: 00. (3時までに家に帰ってください) また、by の後には by the end of April (4月末までに)、by May 10 (5月10日までに)のように月、曜

UNIT 2　GRAMMAR

日、日付などを続けることができます。

2. 時間ではない "by" の用法

「手近にある」→「使える」→「手段」を表す
（例）　I'll go by bus/by car/by plane.

Ⅳ. 前置詞 "up" のイメージ

　up は「上に」という意味だけでなく、横になっている物が「動いて」、「上に向かい」、そして「力尽きるまで連続して動く」、そしてついには「力尽きる」、というイメージです。

① "up" は「動く」、その結果「連続する」、「空間を埋める」
　　He went up to Tokyo. （方面に動いた）
　　My daughter has grown up remarkably. （ますます大きくなっている）

②「～の方に、事が起きて」
　　What's up? （ことが起こる）
　　Which track will the next up train start from? （上り電車）

③「最後まで動作を持続させる」→「尽きる」
　　The meeting broke up. （中断した）
　　The party broke up. （散会した）
　　Finally three houses have burned up. （全焼した）

④ 形容詞＋ up で閉鎖的な連続した状態を示す

I've heard he is hard up for money. （お金に困っている）

⑤ 2者間の空間を埋める

Please come up here. （ここまで来てください）

V．前置詞 "for" のイメージ

1. "for" のイメージと意味

for は「内部、外部の両方向に向かう、向けられる」というイメージです。具体的には「～を求めて」、「～を目的として」、「～に向かう」、「～の期間」などの意味があります。

① 「～のため、～にとって：方向」

　　Is this train for Kobe?　（この電車は神戸方面ですか）

　＊Is this train to Kobe?　（この電車は神戸に行きますか：目的地）

　　These flowers are for you.　（この花はあなたに向けてのものです）

　　What does JR stand for?　（JR は何を表していますか：意味の方向）

② 「～を目的として」

　　I'm looking for a job.　（～を求めて見る→～を探す）

　　I haven't seen you for a long time.　（長い間：～を求めて）

　　I paid five dollars for the book.

　　（その本をに5ドル払いました：～を求めて、～を得るために）

③「賛成・支持」

Are you for or against the plan?

(あなたは、その計画に賛成ですか、反対ですか：～に向かう→賛成)

④「範囲」

He is responsible for quality control.

(彼は品質管理に責任があります：～に向かって、～に対して)

For all I know, he is innocent.

(私の知っている限り、彼は無罪です：～の範囲で)

I've lived here for ten years.

(私はここに10年間住んでいます：～の時間的な範囲で)

2. "for" を含む主な句動詞／熟語

answer for ～ ＝ ～の報いを受ける、　ask for ～ ＝ ～を求める、call for ～ ＝ ～を呼びかける、要求する、　do for ～ ＝ ～の代りになる、fall for ～ ＝ ～にだまされる、　for a long time ＝長い間、　go for ～ ＝ ～を目指す、　head for ～ ＝ ～に向かう、　live for ～ ＝ ～を生きがいにする、　look for ～ ＝ ～を探す、　make for ～ ＝ ～の方向へ進む、～に役立つ、　run for ～ ＝ ～に立候補する、speak for ～ ＝ ～を擁護する、代理で話す、　stand for ～ ＝ ～を表す、work for ～ ＝ ～に勤めている、～に役立つ

VI. 前置詞 "from" と "since" のイメージ

1. 時間を表すとき

どちらも「〜から」と訳すことができますが、次のように用法が異なります。
　from：ある起点を基準にして、そこから離れていくイメージです。この起点が過去、現在、未来のどこでも良い。
　From the age of eleven, I played the piano. （11歳の時から私はピアノを弾きました：起点は「過去」）
　From the age of eleven, I will play the piano. （11歳から私はピアノを弾きます：起点は「未来」）
　since：過去のある時点から現在に至るまで、「動作や状態が継続している」ことを表します。時制は現在完了形、または現在完了進行形となります。現在の代わりに過去や未来の場合もあります。
　Since the age of 22, I have taught/I have been teaching English in this school. （20歳の時から、この学校で英語を教えています）

2. 時間ではない "from" の用法

　ある場所から「離れる」イメージの from は単なる時間的な起点だけではなく、物質的な起点も表します。be made from は「〜から作られる」という物質的な起点、すなわち、「原材料」を表します。
　Wine is made from grapes. （ワインはぶどうから作られる）

Ⅶ. 前置詞 "with" のイメージ

with は2つのものがぶつかって、その後共存する意味合いがあります。

① 「～に対して／～に向かって」

All these girls are in love with Tom.

He is strict with children.

この用法は be familiar with～, be angry with～, be amused with～, be pleased with～, など感情を表わす時によく使われます。

② 「～に関して」

What is the matter with you?

（あなたに関わる問題は何ですか→どうしたんですか）

It's all right with me. （私に関しては大丈夫です→私は大丈夫です）

③ 「～と一緒に」

Will you go out with me ?

（私と一緒に出かけませんか→私と出かけませんか）

Are you with me? （話の内容についてきてますか：精神的なつながり）

④ 「～を持って」

I have no money with me. （私の手元にはお金がありません）

She is a girl with blond hair.

（ブロンドの髪を持っている→ブロンドの髪の）

⑤「時のつながり」

He left home with the door open. （ドアを開けたままで：付帯状況の with）

He is in bed with the flu.

（インフルエンザが原因で～：原因・結果のつながり）

Ⅷ. 前置詞 "behind" と "beyond" のイメージ

1. "behind" のイメージと意味

behind は「場所の後ろ／物の後ろ」、転じて「後ろから支える」イメージで、「～を味方して」、「～を支持して」などの意味になります。

There was a small village behind the hill.

（丘の向こうに小さな村がありました）

Party members will always unite behind their leaders.

（党員はいつも党首を支持して結束を固めるものだ）

2. "beyond" のイメージと意味

beyond は「時間や場所を超えた向こう側」のイメージから転じて、「限界を超えた」のような比喩的な用法もあります。

I went three stations beyond my destination.

（私は駅を3つ乗り越してしまいました）

The beauty of Mt. Aso is beyond description.

（阿蘇山の美しさは言い尽くせません）

UNIT 2　GRAMMAR

Ⅸ. 前置詞 "in" と "into" のイメージ

in は「（入れ物）の中に／で」という動きを表します。into は in + to で「（入れ物）の中へ向かって入って行く」という「動き」を表します。

You have to jump in the swimming pool. （あなたはプールという入れ物の中で跳ばなくてはならない→あなたはプールで跳ばなくてはならない、あなたはプールで跳びこまなければならない）この例文の場合、jum into が jump in と同様に使われることもあります。

You have to jump into the pool. （あなたはプールという入れ物の中に向かって飛び込まなくてはならない→あなたはプールの中に（高いところから）飛びこまなければならない）この場合は jump in とはなりません。前者の例文が「プールの中で飛び込みをする」ことを意味するのに対し、後者の例文は「プールの中に飛び込む」ことを意味します。

① "in" の例文

In my opinion, he is very smart.　私の意見を「抽象的な入れ物」と考えて、「私の意見の中で」即ち、「私の意見では」という意味を表しています。

Tom walked in the park.　（トムは公園の中を歩きました）

Mary was running in the field.　（メアリーはグランド内を走っています）

I'm in good health.　この文では「いい健康の中」即ち、「健康だ」の意味になります。

② "into" の例文

Tom got off the bus, and hurried into the office.

（トムはバスを降りて、事務所に急いで入りました）

The rain turned into snow last night. （昨晩雨は雪に変わりました）
turn（変わる）に into がつくと「赤という状態に向かって変わる」即ち、「赤に変わる」という意味になります。このように into は「〜の状態へと変化する」時にも使われます。

Ⅹ. 前置詞 "above" と "below" のイメージ

「ある一定の基準の上方にある」ことを表すときは above を、「ある一定の基準の下方にある」ことを示すときは below を使います。

① "above" の例文
The temperature has not risen much above zero for the past three days.
（気温は最近3日間0℃から上にさほど上がってない）　ここでは0℃が基準になっています。

② "below" の例文
The sun goes down below the horizon. （太陽は地平線の下に沈む）
基準は地平線となっています。

Ⅺ. 前置詞 "over" と "under" のイメージ

ある物が「表面に接触しないで離れていて（真）上にある」ことを表す時は over を、「表面に接触しないで離れていて（真）下にある」ことを表す時に under を使います。

① "over" の例文

The cat jumped over the fence.
（猫は塀の真上を飛び越えた→猫は塀を飛び越えた）

② "under" の例文

The cat is sleeping under the table.
（猫がテーブルの真下で眠っている→猫がテーブルの下で眠っている）
He is under me. （彼は私の下にいる→彼は私の部下です）

XII. 前置詞 "on" と "over" のイメージ

「X．前置詞 "over" と "under" のイメージ」でも取り上げた over と on はどちらも「〜の上にある」という場所を表す前置詞ですが、次のような違いがあります。

1. 接触を表す "on"

　表面に接触していれば全て on を使います。「上に接している」だけでなく、例えば、天井の「下に接している」場合でも、あるいは壁の「側面に接している」場合でも on を使います。
The cat is on the roof. （猫は屋根と接している→猫は屋根にいる）
My work is on the ceiling.
（私の作品は天井に接している→私の作品は天井にある）
The clock is hanging on the wall.
（時計は壁に接してかかっている→時計は壁にかかっている）

2. 接触を表さない "over"

　over は「表面に接しておらず、上にある」時に使います。しばしば「～の真上ある」ことを表します。

　The moon is over the river.　moon（月）は川の水面からはるか上方にあり、水面とは接触していません。

　He is over me.　（彼は私の上にいる→彼は私の上司です）

　He traveled all over the world.　ここの over は「全体を覆って」の意味合いがあります。all がついているので「世界全体を覆って」から「世界中」の意味になります。

Part 2

Understanding Phrasal Verbs
―句動詞の理解―

UNIT 2　GRAMMAR

Ⅰ．句動詞とは？

　英文の主要素は主語、動詞、目的語、補語があり、中でも動詞が最重要であることは言うまでもありません。前著"Cross-cultural Studies through English — 異文化学のすすめ —"の中で、これらの要素については詳述しましたので、本書では、これをさらに深めて、動詞の中でも特に重要と思われる「句動詞」（phrasal verbs）に焦点を当てたいと思います。「句動詞」はあまり聞きなれない言葉ですが、別名「群動詞」または「動詞句」と言われています。句動詞は主に「基本動詞＋前置詞」または「基本動詞＋副詞」で構成されています。

　本書では、主な基本動詞、また、それらと共に用いられている前置詞のイメージに焦点を当てます。なぜなら、この前置詞のイメージを理解することによって、基本動詞の本来の意味から変化した、新しい句動詞の意味を推測できるからです。

Ⅱ．句動詞の基本概念

1.「句動詞」

　「句動詞」は「動詞＋前置詞」または「動詞＋副詞」で、一つの動詞のような働きをするものです。英会話に使用される約7割は約100個の動詞でできています。さらには、その100語の中で約2割が基本的な動詞(be, have, do, say, make, take, get, give, go, see, put)だと言われています。これらの基本動詞が頻出する一つの理由としては、それらが単独で出てくるのみではなく「句動詞」という形で出てくるからです。たとえば、go back は「家に帰る」、go beyond～は「～にまさる」、go for～は「～にする」、go for it は「頑張れ」などの意味になります。goが

「行く」という基本の意味で使われる以外に、その基本動詞に続く前置詞や副詞などのイメージによって、全く新しい意味の句動詞が成立するからです。言い換えると、「句動詞」とは次の3つの条件を満たしているものと言うことができます。

① 「基本動詞＋前置詞」または「基本動詞＋副詞」で構成されている。
② 組み合わさることによって、それぞれの単語が持つ意味とは違う内容になる。
③ 単語の数は2語～3語である。

The World cup will come around next year in Japan.
（ワールドカップは、来年日本にやってくる予定です）
I stayed up all night watching the Olympics.
（一晩中起きて、オリンピックを見ていました）
stay（留まる）、up（上へ）というそれぞれの意味と関係のない、stay up（起きている、徹夜する）という新しい意味となっている。これが「句動詞」です。しかし、もともとの単語の持つ意味が変わってない場合は「句動詞」とは呼びません。それは単なる「動詞＋前置詞」あるいは「動詞＋副詞」なので注意してください。ただし、動詞によっては「句動詞」か、または、動詞を含む「熟語」かの区別が難しい時があります。この時は上記の3つの条件を満たしているかどうかで判断するしかないようです。

2. 基本動詞

ここで言う基本動詞とは、その動詞が後ろに前置詞か副詞を伴って、一つの句動詞を構成するための基本となる動詞のことです。基本動詞には自動詞または他動詞がなります。さらには句動詞も一体となって自動詞または他動詞の働き

をします。

3.「句動詞」の種類

① 「自動詞＋前置詞」で、1個の他動詞と同じ意味になる。
People never <u>thought of</u> such plans.
（人々はそんな計画<u>を考えた</u>ことはありませんでした）
　文中、下線部 thought of は自動詞 thought (think の過去形) が、of という前置詞を伴って「～を思いつく、～を考える」という一つの他動詞の意味を持つようになっています。

look at ～ = ～を見る、 depend on ～ = ～を頼りにする、 consist of ～ = ～から成る、 speak to ～ = ～に話しかける、 believe in ～ = ～の正しいことを信じる、 agree with ～ = ～に同意する、 wish for ～ = ～を希望する

② 「自動詞＋副詞」で、1個の他動詞と同じ意味になる。
<u>make up</u> one's mind = 決心する　　<u>give up</u> smoking = 喫煙をやめる

③ 「自動詞＋副詞＋前置詞」で、1個の他動詞と同じ意味になる。
<u>make up for</u> the mistake =過ちを償う　<u>look down upon</u> him =彼を軽蔑する
<u>look up to</u> her =彼女を尊敬する　<u>make up with</u> the neighbor = 近所の人と仲直りする

1) Could you <u>turn on</u> the light?　（ライトをつけてくださいませんか）
2) Could you <u>turn</u> the light <u>on</u>?
3) Could you turn it on?

　1)、2) は同じ意味です。

　turn は本来、他動詞ですから例文 2) のように（他動詞＋目的語＋副詞）の語順となり、目的語(the light)を他動詞のすぐ後に持ってくることができます。また、例文 1) のように（他動詞＋副詞＋目的語）も可能です。

　1) と 2) でどちらの文を使うかは、文全体のリズムの好みによります。しかし、例文 3) のように目的語が代名詞の場合には turn it on と「他動詞＋目的語＋副詞」のように例文 2) の語順にし、例文 3) のようになります。

④　名詞を伴う句動詞
1)「他動詞＋名詞」で 1 個の自動詞の意味になる。
　When is the sports day going to <u>take place</u>?　（運動会はいつ<u>行われますか</u>）
2)「他動詞＋名詞＋前置詞」で 1 個の他動詞の意味になる。
　I'll <u>take advantage of</u> these special prices.　（この特別価格を<u>利用します</u>）

4.　紛らわしい「句動詞」

①　同じ動詞が「句動詞」の中で自動詞にも他動詞にも使われる時、即ち
　「自動詞＋前置詞」か「他動詞＋副詞」かが分かりにくい時があります。
1) I'll <u>get off</u> the train at the next station.　（私は次の駅で電車を<u>降ります</u>）
　この get は「～へ動く」という意の自動詞に off という前置詞を伴って「～を降りる」という他動詞になっています。そのため、get と off を分けることはできません。よって、I'll get the bus off. とは言えません。

UNIT 2　GRAMMAR

2) You will never get back the money.　（そのお金を返してもらうのは無理です）

　　上記の文では You will never get the money back. と言えるので back が副詞だと分かります。副詞は比較的自由に場所を変えることができます。また、この文の get はその直後に目的語を伴うことができるので、他動詞だと分かります。

② 「句動詞」中にある前置詞と副詞の見分け方

　　他動詞や前置詞は目的語を必要としますが、副詞は目的語を必要とせず、また、文中での位置も比較的自由です。これらの性質を理解して下記例文中の on, up などが前置詞か、それとも副詞かを考えて見ましょう。

1) I called up Elley last night.　（私は昨晩エリーに電話しました）

　　この場合 call という動詞が自動詞か他動詞かが問題となります。その見分け方は call という動詞の後にきている語（ここでは up）を Elley の後に移動しても文意が成り立つかどうかです。すなわち、I called Elley up last night. が成り立つかどうかです。この書き換えは成立しますので、この up は副詞となります。なぜなら、副詞は文中での語順が比較的自由なこと、そして、動詞のすぐ後に目的語を必要としないからです。また文中の call はすぐ後に Elley を目的語として持つこともできるので、他動詞と分かります。

2) I called on Elley last night.　（私は昨晩エリーさんを訪れました）

　　この文を I called Elley on last night. と書き換えることはできません。I called Elley last night. にして（昨夜エリーさんに電話した）の意味なら可能ですが on があるので、I called Elley on last night. は不可能な文です。 call on は2語で1つの他動詞となって Elley という目的語を持っています。よって文中の on は前置詞であり call という自動詞を「句動詞」として他動詞に変えています。

5. 自動詞と他動詞の留意点

① 自動詞の中には、そのまま他動詞としても用いられるものがあります。原則として「～する」という意味の自動詞に、「～させる」という使役の意味を加えたものです。

（自動詞） The door opened. （ドアが開いた）
（他動詞） I opened the door. （私はドアを開けた）

② 同一の動作や状態を表わすために、場合によっては自動詞を用いたり他動詞を用いたりします。もちろん、この二つの表現が、まったく等しいというわけではなく、その間にいくぶんかの相違がありますが、実際に表現される動作の本質は変わりません。

（他動詞） I <u>see</u> a bird. （見る）
（自動詞） I <u>look</u> at a bird. （見る）

（他動詞） I <u>hear</u> a song. （聞く）
（自動詞） I <u>listen</u> to a song. （聞く）

（他動詞） We <u>respect</u> her. （尊敬する）
（自動詞） We <u>look</u> up to her. （尊敬する）

③ 日本語の意味から自動詞、他動詞の区別をすると誤ることがあります。
1) 日本語の自動詞が、英語では他動詞になる場合。
（東京<u>に着く</u>）
× reach to Tokyo   ○ <u>reach</u> Tokyo

UNIT 2　GRAMMAR

（東京から離れる）
× leave from Tokyo　　○　leave Tokyo

2) 日本語の他動詞が、英語では自動詞になる場合。

（東京を出発する）
× start Tokyo　　　　○　start from Tokyo

（道路を走る）
× run a road　　　　○　run on a road

（歌を聞く）
× listen a song　　　○　listen to a song

Ⅲ.「句動詞」の実際
　　— Go, Come, Put, Run, Speak, Talk, Say, Tell, Look, Get, Call, Bring —

◎　基本動詞 "Go"

1. "Go" の用法

① 自動詞としての用法
・　行く、進む、動く、（職業などに）就く
　　go to the bar　（弁護士になる）

② 他動詞としての用法
・　（通例否定文で）～に耐える
　　I can't go the noise.　（その騒音に耐えられません）
・　（金を）賭ける

I'll go a dollar on the race. （そのレースに1ドル賭けます）

③ 名詞としての用法
1) 行くこと　　the come and go of the tide　（潮の満ち引き）
2) 元気　　　 He is full of go.　（彼は元気いっぱいだ）
3) 機会、試み　have a go　（試して使ってみる）

④ 形容詞としての用法
・（システムなどが）用意できて
　Thunderbirds are go!　（サンダーバード出動準備完了： 用意ができて）

2. "Go" を使った句動詞

go through = examine,　　go up = increase,　　go with = accompany,　　go on = continue,　　go over = check,　　go through = experience,　　go into = get a job,　　go off = explode,　　go for = do, enjoy,　　go for it = try,　　go back = return,　　go beyond = surpass,　　go by = pass by

3. "Go" を使った句動詞／熟語の練習問題

UNIT 2　GRAMMAR

問題：　日本文に合うように、次の "Go" の句動詞／熟語の（　）内に適切な語を次の語群から選び、英文を完成させなさい。

1. そのドレスは靴に合います。

    The dress goes (　　　　) my shoes.

2. 冷たくなるから、先に始めて下さい。

    Go (　　　　) and start before everything gets cold.

3. 彼女は彼と一緒にパーティーに行きたがっています。

    She wants to go (　　　　) to the party with him.

4. それは私たちの想像をはるかに上回る結果だった。

    It went quite well (　　　　) our expectations.

5. 時がたって、僕はもう高校3年生ですよ。

    The time went (　　　　), and I'm already a senior in high school.

6. 散歩に行きませんか。

    Shall we go (　　　　) a walk?

7. 卒業後は看護師になりたいです。

    I want to go (　　　　) nursing after college.

8. 突然に爆発が起こった。

    All of a sudden, the bomb went (　　　　).

9. 会議は思ったより長引いてしまった。

    The meeting went (　　　　) longer than I expected.

10. 君の提出した課題について話し合いましょう。

    Let's go (　　　　) the reports you turned in.

（語群）　with,　　on,　　for,　　off,　　over,　　into,　　beyond,　　ahead,　　along,　　by

（奇数番号の解答）
1. with,　　3. along,　　5. by,　　7. into,　　9. on

4. "Go" に関する「話の泉」

"Go" を使った表現：　Be gone　（なくなる）
go は「今いるところから別の場所へはなれていく」の意味なので go の過去分詞の gone を用いると「別の場所に行ってしまった」、あるいは「～がなくなった」という意味になります。

時々、「私は京都に行ったことがあります」と言いたい時に、I have gone to Kyoto. という方がいますが「今ここに、いない人が、ここで話すことができないので誤りです。I have been to Kyoto. が正解です（ただし、アメリカ英語では、gone でも良くなりつつあります）。

もう一つ例を出しましょう。 My stomachache is gone.（私の腹痛は別の場所に行ってしまった／私の腹痛は消えた）という意味になります。

◎　基本動詞 "Come"

1. "Come" の用法

come「来る」 go「行く」とだけ丸暗記するのではなく、「話し手の視点」によって考えることが大切です。

I'm coming.　（今、そちらに行きます／今、そちらに向かいます）
I'm going.　（行ってきます　＊話し相手のところに行くのではありません）

UNIT 2　GRAMMAR

- come home と go home の違い

一見すると、どちらも「家に帰る」という同じ意味に思えますが、視点が違います。come は「今いる場所から別の場所へ離れて行く」というイメージです。

1) I came home from my office at 9:00.
　（事務所を出て9時に家に着いた）　事務所を出た時間は不明
2) I went home from my office at 9:00.
　（9時に事務所を出て、家に向かった）　家に着いた時間は不明

2. "Come" を使った「句動詞」

come up = approach, arise, be on one's way,　　come up with = think of, hit on, come with = include, require,　come out = be published, appear,　come on = develop, hurry,　come off = remove, fall,　come into = inherit, become, come in = enter,　come from = belong to, be born in,　come back = recur, come across = encounter, appear,　come along = appear, progress, hurry

3. "Come" を含む句動詞の練習問題

Part 2 Understanding Phrasal Verbs ― 句動詞の理解 ―

問題： 日本語に合うように、次の"Come"の句動詞の(　)内に適切な語を次の語群から選び、英文を完成させなさい。ただし、日本語は現在形の意味である。

1. I (　　　　　) a friend　　（～に偶然会う= come on　～, encounter　～）
2. You go ahead. I'll (　　　　　).　（追いかける= follow）
3. The snow (　　　　　).　　（降る= fall, pour）
4. Tom (　　　　　) a rich family.　（～の生まれだ= belong to ~）
5. Does the word "tsunami" (　　　　　) the Japanese language?
   （～に由来する　= derive from～）
6. Can you believe that I (　　　　　) first?　（入賞する　=win a prize）
7. The dirt on my shirt is not (　　　　　).　（(汚れが)落ちる= be removed）
8. Hey,(　　　　　), we don't have much time to lose.（早くしなさい= hurry up）
9. Why don't you (　　　　　)?　（立ち寄る= visit）
10. He (　　　　　) a good idea.　（～を思いつく= think of　～）

（語群）　come over,　　came in,　　came across,　　come from,
coming off,　come on,　came from,　came up with,　come along,
came down

（奇数番号の解答）

1. came across, 3. came down, 5. come from, 7. coming off, 9. come over

4. "Come" に関する「話の泉」

・ come と go に対する英語と日本語の発想の違い

「あなたのところに行きます。」I'll come to you. で I'll go to you. とは言いません。換言しますと英語で二人が話す時、基準になる人は話を聞いている相手と言うことです。相手から見れば、あなたは話し相手に向かって、やって来るのです。よって、come という発想になるようです。

go という動詞は会話中の2人のいる場所以外に話し手が行く時に用います。

I'll go to see him tomorrow. （明日、彼に会いに行きます）

なお、come and see = come to see は「ぜひ～して下さい」のような招待の気持ちを示す時に使います。

You must come and see us when you come to Japan.
（日本に来られたら、ぜひ我が家にいらしてください）

◎ 基本動詞 "Put"

1. "Put" の用法

① 自動詞としての用法

1)（船などが）進む、向かう(put back/put in/put out)、（河水などが）流れて行く、走る

The ship put back to port. （その船は港に戻った）

2) 退去する

The man suddenly put for home.

（その男の人は突然帰宅した）

② 他動詞としての用法
1) （ある場所に）置く、据える、載せる、入れる、投ずる、加える、横たえる

He put a wallet in the pocket. （彼は財布をポケットに入れた）
2) （ある場所に）持っていく、課す、〜のせいにする

She put her failure on me. （彼女は自分の失敗を私のせいにした）

③ 名詞としての用法
1) （砲丸などの）投げ、投てき、押し
2) [証券] 売りつけ選択権、プットオプション（put option）（特定の証券を売る権利）

2. "Put" を使った「句動詞」

put には次のような句動詞／熟語があります。同じ句動詞でも、文脈で意味が異なる時がありますが、代表的な意味は次のようなものです。

put across = やり遂げる、　　put ahead = 進ませる、　　put aside = 脇へ置く、
put by = 蓄える、　　put forth = 出航する、　　put it over = ごまかす、
put off = 延期する、　　put on = 身につける、　　put through = やり遂げる、
put it another way = 別の言い方をする、　　put together = 集める、
put out = 消す、　　put down = 書きとめる、　　put up = 掲示する、泊る

3. "Put" を使った句動詞の練習問題

UNIT 2 GRAMMAR

問題： 日本文に合うように、次の"Put"の句動詞の(　)内に適切な語を次の語群から選び、英文を完成させなさい。

1. 僕は試験終了時に鉛筆を置かなかった。
    I didn't put the pencil (　　　) when the examination was over.
2. 1つ間違えただけなのに、彼は皆の前で私をけなした。
    He put me (　　　) in front of everyone for one mistake.
3. 外は寒い。コートでも着たら。
    It's cold outside. Why don't you put (　　　) a coat?
4. よく見えるために、電気でもつけたら。
    Why don't you put (　　　) the light so you can see better?
5. そうだね。彼女は去年で5キロ太ったって。
    I know. She said she put (　　　) 5kg last year.
6. 寝る前には必ず電気を消すのですよ。
    Make sure you put (　　　) the light before you go to sleep.
7. 壁に張る写真をまとめているんだ。
    I'm putting (　　　) the pictures to put on the wall.
8. はい。終末は泊めてあげるよ。
    No problem. I'll put you (　　　) for the weekend.
9. 答えが分かる人は手を上げて下さい。
    Put (　　　) your hand if you know the answer.
10. そんなの耐えられませんよ。家に帰りたいです。
    I can't put (　　　) with it! I want to go home.

(語群)   on,   up,   down,   together,   off
＊複数回使用するものがあります

(奇数番号の解答)
1. down,　　3. on,　　5. on,　　7. together,　　9. up

4. "Put" に関する「話の泉」

・ put on と wear の違い
　put on は(〜を身につける)動作を示し wear は(〜を身につけている)状態を示します。

1) I'm putting on a red tie.
例文は、「今赤いネクタイをつけようとしている」という動作を示しています。

2) I always wear a red tie.
例文は、「赤いネクタイをつけている」という状態を示しています。

1) You should put on your coat.

2) You should wear your coat.

どちらも正しい文ですが、ニュアンスは以下のようになります。

1) (外は寒いから)ここでコートを着た方がいいよ。

2) (外は寒いから)コートを着たままの方がいいよ。

◎ 基本動詞 "Run"

1. "Run" の用法

① 自動詞としての用法
1) 走る、逃げる、競争に出る
　Sally came running past at top speed.　(サリーさんは全速力で走り去った)

UNIT 2　GRAMMAR

2)（機械などが）動く、（道などが）延びている

The road runs along the coast.　（道路は海岸にそって延びている）

② 他動詞としての用法

1)（道路などで）遊ぶ

Children run the streets.　（子どもたちが通りで遊ぶ）

2)（競争を）する

I'll run a race with her.　（私は彼女と競争するつもりです）

3) 経営する

He is running a karaoke bar.　（彼はカラオケ店を経営している）

2. "Run" を使った「句動詞」

run through = glance at, consume, rehearse,　　run out of = use up, exhaust,
run out = expire,　　run on =go on,　　run down = use up, exhaust,
run into = meet ～ by chance, collide with,　　run away = escape,
run across= meet ～ by chance

3. "Run" を使った句動詞の練習問題

Part 2 Understanding Phrasal Verbs — 句動詞の理解 —

問題： 日本文に合うように、次の"Run"の句動詞の(　　)内に適切な語を次の語群から選び、英文を完成させなさい。

1. 君はその問題から逃げているよ。
    You are (　　　　　　　　) the problem.
2. 彼女は家出したんです。
    She (　　　　　　　　) home.
3. 現実から目を背けないようにしましょう。
    Let's not (　　　　　　　　) reality.
4. ヘッドライトを消して下さいよ、でないとバッテリーが上がってしまいますよ。
    Switch off your headlights, or you'll (　　　　　　　　) the battery.
5. トラックがいつなんどき通りで私の自転車に衝突するかもしれない。
    A truck may (　　　　　　　　) my bicycle in the street anytime.
6. 僕は渋谷で中学校の時の圭君に偶然会ったよ。
    I (　　　　　　　　) Kei from junior high school at Shibuya.
7. ミーテイングが長引いて、たった今出てきたところです。
    The meeting (　　　　　　　　), and I just got out now.
8. 私のパスポートが切れたのに気付かなかった。
    I didn't realize that my passport (　　　　　　　　).
9. それは単なるガス欠ですよ。
    It simply (　　　　　　　　) gas.
10. もう一度、その計画の詳細をざっと見てみましょう。
    Let's (　　　　　　　　) the details of the plan again.

（語群）　run down,　ran on,　ran out,　run away from,　ran away from　run into,　ran out of,　ran into,　run through,　running away from

UNIT 2　GRAMMAR

（奇数番号の解答）
1. running away from,　　3. run away from,　　5. run into,　　7. ran on,
9. ran out of

4.　"Run" に関する「話の泉」

　今回は、ビジネスの社会で役に立つ英文例のクイズです。「　　　」内の日本語を英語にする時、あなたなら、どちらの英文を使いますか？

①「ボスが変わりました」
1) I have a new boss.　　　2) My boss changed.
　1) が正解です。2) では（ボスの性格が変わった）という意味です。日本語では主語の省略や受動態と能動態の用法があいまいなので、2) のような文を考えてしまうようです。

②「時間通りにお願いします」
1) You need to be on time.　　　2) You had better be on time.
　1) が正解です。2) も文法的には誤りではありませんが、had better は上から目線の文ですから、状況を考えて使いましょう。

③「田中は1月10日までお休みをいただいております」
1) Mr. Tanaka is on vacation until January 10.
2) Tanaka is on vacation until January 10.
　日本では社内の人間を「田中」と敬称なしで呼びますが、ネイティブには「田中ってやつ」と聞こえます。ここでは Mr./Ms.をつけるか、ファーストネームで呼ぶと自然です。

Part 2 Understanding Phrasal Verbs — 句動詞の理解 —

◎ 基本動詞 "Speak, Talk, Say, Tell"

1. "Speak, Talk, Say, Tell" の用法

① "Speak" の意味と用法
　口から一方的に音を出すことを表し、演説のようなもので、話が「一方通行」であることが多いです。

　Speak to me. （何か私に話してください）
　Could you speak slowly? （ゆっくり話してくださいませんか）
　May I speak to Hanako? （花子さんと話せますか）
　Speak up. I can't hear you. （大きな声で話してください。聞こえませんよ）
　Speaking of Nishikori, he is a great tennis player.
　（錦織と言えば、彼はすごいテニスプレヤーです）
　Do you know her? I know her by name, but not to speak to.
　（彼女を知ってますか。話したことはないけれど、名前は知ってますよ）

② "Talk" の意味と用法
　いつも話し相手がいる。→皆で話し合う。

　What are you talking about? （何を話しているの）
　You were talking in your sleep.
　（夢の中で相手と話していましたよ→寝言を言っていましたよ）
　Money talks. （お金がものを言う）
　I talked with my mother about family affairs. （母と家事について話しました）

UNIT 2　GRAMMAR

③ "Say" の意味と用法

　話す内容に重点があります。Say "OK" to him. （彼に "OK" と言いなさい）は可ですが、Speak "OK" to him. は不可です。Speak では話の内容は述べられることはありません。Say something. （何か言ってくださいよ）では、something が話の内容になります。

The weather forecast says that it will snow tomorrow.
　（明日雪が降るでしょう）が話す内容となります。
The letter says that Tom is doing well.
　（トムは頑張っている）が話の内容となります。

④ "Tell" の意味と用法
相手に情報を伝える→情報伝達

He told me the good news. （いいニュースを話してくれました）
Could you tell me the way to the station? （駅への道を教えてくれますか）
Don't tell me you forgot the room key. （まさか部屋のカギを忘れたんですか）
Don't tell a lie. （嘘を言わないで）
He told a joke. （彼は冗談を言った）

2. "Speak" を使った句動詞／熟語

speak ill of ～ = ～の悪口を言う、　speak well of ～ = ～をほめる、
speaking of ～ = ～と言えば、　speak up = はっきり話す、発言する、
speak to ～ = ～に話しかける

3. "Speak" を使った句動詞／熟語の練習問題

問題： 日本語に合うように、次の"Speak"の句動詞／熟語の（　）内に適切な語を次の語群から選び、英文を完成させなさい。ただし、日本語は現在形、能動態の意味である。

1. Takeshi (　　　　　　) my school.　（演説をする）
2. I can't (　　　　　　) her.　（〜をかばう）
3. He (　　　　　　) today's world economy.　（〜について話す）
4. We need to (　　　　　　).　（はっきり意見を言う）
5. I was (　　　　　　) by a stranger.　（〜に話しかける）
6. (　　　　　　). I can't hear you.　（大声で話す）
7. Could you (　　　　　　) Keiko for me.　（〜と話す）
8. (　　　　　　) sports, I like tennis.　（〜と言えば）
9. You should not (　　　　　　) others.　（〜の悪口を言う）
10. He can speak French, not to (　　　　　　) English.
    （〜は言うまでもなく）

（語群）　speak with,　　speak up for,　　Speaking of,　　speak of,　　speak ill of,　　spoke at,　　Speak up,　　speak up,　　spoken to,　　spoke on

UNIT 2　GRAMMAR

（奇数番号の解答）
1. spoke at,　　3. spoke on,　　5. spoken to,　　7. speak with,　　9. speak ill of

4. "Speak" に関する「話の泉」

"Speaking of which"（ところで）、ここでよく受ける質問についてお話しします。

① be going to と will の違い
簡単に言いますと次のような違いがあります。
　be going to ～ は主語の a)「予定」または b)「意図」に関する時を表す場合に用います。will ～ は主語の c)「思いつき」または「その場の判断」を表す場合に用います。
1)　What are you going to do today?　（今日は何をする予定ですか）
2)　What are you going to eat here?　（何をお召し上がりですか）
3)　I'll be back.　（すぐに戻って来ます）

② be going to と will の違いに関するクイズ
　次の文 1)、2) のうち、玄関のベルに応じる時の英語はどちらでしょうか。
1)　I'll get the door.
2)　I'm going to get the door.
ヒント:「玄関のベルが鳴る」のは、予定それとも突然？
正解は 1) です。

◎ 基本動詞 "Look"

1. " Look " の用法

① 自動詞としての用法
1) 見る： I'm just looking. （見ているだけです）
2) 見える：You look wonderful in this hat. （この帽子よく似合ってますよ）
   この場合、形容詞の wonderful は補語です。

② 他動詞としての用法
1) 見る： Look me in the eye. （私の目を見てください）

③ 名詞としての用法
1) 見ること、一見、一目、外観 ： He has his mother's look.
   （彼は母親に似ている）
   look という基本動詞の用法は多くあるので「句動詞」も多くあります。

2. "Look " を使用した句動詞

look after = take care of,　　look around = browse,　　look back on = remember,　　look for = search for,　　look forward to = anticipate,　　look into = investigate,　　look on = watch, consider,　　look up to= respect,　　look down on =despise

3. "Look" を使った句動詞の練習問題

UNIT 2　GRAMMAR

問題：日本文に合うように、次の"Look"の句動詞の(　　)内に適切な語を次の語群から選び、英文を完成させなさい。

1. 大丈夫。僕が面倒みるから。
    Don't worry! I'll look (　　　　) them.
2. 中を見て回りますか。
    Would you like to look (　　　　) inside?
3. 壁に掛けられたあの絵をご覧ください。
    Would you look (　　　　) that painting on the wall?
4. 彼はハーバードでMBAを取ってからとんとん拍子だったな。
    He never looked (　　　　) after getting an MBA at Harvard.
5. 鍵を探してるんだが、そうでないと出かけることができないんだ。
    I'm looking (　　　　) my keys, or else I can't go out.
6. イタリアで君に会うのを楽しみにしてますよ。
    I'm looking (　　　　) to seeing you in Italy.
7. もっと細かく調べる必要があるよ。
    We need to look (　　　　) the matter more carefully.
8. 他の連中は黙って見ていただけさ。
    The rest of them just looked (　　　　) in silence.
9. 彼はその光景から目をそらした。
    He looked (　　　　) from the scene.
10. 私は暗がりの中を見ようとしたが、何も見えなかった。
    I looked (　　　　) the dark but saw nothing.

（語群）　on,　forward,　after,　at,　back,　into,　around,　for,　away,　in

（奇数番号の解答）
1. after,　　3. at,　　5. for,　　7. into,　　9. away

4. "Look" に関する「話の泉」

　"Looking back on my own experience,"（自分自身の経験を振り返って）、英語で良く使われる please について述べてみます。please には①「喜ばせる」（動詞）と、②「どうぞ」（間投詞）という意味があります。

①の例文　She is hard to please.
　　（彼女は喜ばせるのが難しい→彼女は気難しい）

②の例文　Please enter the house.　（どうぞ部屋にお入りください）
　　　　　　Please have a seat.　（おかけください）

・相手が困る please の例
○ Please give me coffee.　（コーヒーをください）
× Please get me coffee.　（コーヒーをくれ）
　もともと乱暴な文に please がつくのは不自然です。

◎　基本動詞 "Get"

1. "Get" の用法

　get には「得る/ 達する」など自動詞と他動詞の両方で多くの意味があります。

UNIT 2　GRAMMAR

この基本動詞が前置詞や副詞と組み合わさると、より多彩な意味になります。
get into ～ ＝ ～に巻き込まれる、～に夢中になる、　　get at ～ ＝ ～に到達する、　get over ～ ＝ ～を乗り越える、～を克服する、
get within ～ ＝ ～の範囲内に入る、　get to ～ ＝ ～に着く、
get on with ～ ＝ ～と仲よくする、　get through to ～ ＝
～と電話がつながる

・　get out of と get out の違い

　Get out of here !　二人は同じ場所にいて、相手に対して「中から出ていけ」の意味になります。

　Get out here !　あなたは外にいて、中の相手に「こちらに出て来い」の意味です。

2．"Get" を使用した句動詞の留意点

　Get out of <u>your car</u> with your hands up!　（手を挙げて車から出てください）
下線部には乗り物などの名詞が来ます。
　I'll get off <u>the bus</u> at the next station.　（次の駅でバスを降ります）
get は「動く」という意味の自動詞なので、get the bus off の語順は不可です。
　You will never get back the money.　（お金は決して戻って来ないでしょう）
get は「得る」という意味の他動詞なので、get the money back という語順も可です。

3．"Get" を使った句動詞／熟語の練習問題

Part 2 Understanding Phrasal Verbs ― 句動詞の理解 ―

問題： 日本語に合うように、次の"Get"の句動詞の(　)内に適切な語を次の語群から選び、英文を完成させなさい。ただし、日本語は現在形の意味である。

1. He (　　　　　) from reality. （逃れる= escape）
2. He (　　　　　) from a business trip. （帰って来る= return）
3. The plane didn't (　　　　　) on time. （到着する= come）
4. Tom (　　　　　) a taxi yesterday. （〜に乗る= ride）
5. Mary (　　　　　) music. （〜に夢中になる= go in for, enjoy）
6. I'm (　　　　　) in America from tomorrow.
    （休む、休暇をとる= take off）
7. She always (　　　　　) the bus when she is in a hurry.
    （〜に乗車する= board）
8. Does your wife (　　　　　) your mother?
    （〜と仲良くする= get along with 〜）
9. I usually (　　　　　) before six. （起きる≒wake up）
10. I finally (　　　　　) to her on her mobile phone.
    （電話がつながる= connect）

(語群)　gets on,　　got through,　　get up,　　got into,
get on with,　　get in,　　got away,　　getting off,　　got in,
got back

UNIT 2　GRAMMAR

（奇数番号の解答）
1. got away,　3. get in,　5. got into,　7. gets on,　9. get up

4. "Get" に関する「話の泉」

　get out of ～（～から出ていく）という句動詞でも使用されますが、日本人が一番よく使う前置詞の一つは of だ と言われています。なぜなら日本人は of の後に来る名詞との関係を考えずに、日本語の（～の）とくればいつでも of を使用するからです。

① I ate Sushi in Osaka.　（大阪で、お寿司を食べました）
② I ate Sushi of Osaka.　（大阪で作られたお寿司を食べました）

　例文①の in Osaka の前置詞 in は（～の中で）のように場所を表しています。例文②の前置詞 of は「関連性」または「そのものの一部」を表すイメージです。よって、例文②のお寿司は大阪で作られたお寿司で、どこで食べても（大阪のお寿司）なのです。では、下のクイズをやってみてください。

・次の（　）内にはどのような前置詞が入りますか。
1) This glass is made (　　) sand.　（このガラスは砂<u>から</u>できている）
2) This dress is made (　　) linen.　（このドレスは麻<u>から</u>できている）
3) They make grapes (　　　) wine.　（彼らはぶどうをワインにする→ぶどうはワインになる）

正解： 1) from（形が変化するときは from「～から」を使用します）
2) of（of には「～から」という意味があります。ただし、材質が変化しない時です）
3) into（ぶどうからワインにするので結果を表す「into」(～に) が入ります）

◎ 基本動詞 "Call"

1. "Call" の用法

① 他動詞としての用法
call out（叫ぶ、呼びだす）、call in（電話を入れる、呼び出す）、call for（要求する、求める）、目的格補語を伴って call… ～（…を～と名づける）

② 自動詞としての用法
call to ～ ＝ ～に呼びかける、call at（場所）＝ ～に立ち寄る、
call on（人）＝ ～のところに立ち寄る、など

③ 名詞としてのの用法
呼び声、点呼、立ち寄ること、要求、など

2. "Call" を使った句動詞／熟語の練習問題

UNIT 2 GRAMMAR

問題： 日本語に合うように、次の"Call"の句動詞／熟語の（　　）内に適切な語を次の語群から選び、英文を完成させなさい。ただし、日本語は現在形、能動態の意味である。

1. They (　　　　　) his resignation.
   （彼らは彼の退職を要求しました： ～を要求する=require）
2. I (　　　　　) with complaints.
   （私は苦情の電話をかけました： 電話をかける= phone）
3. We will (　　　　　) the candidate.
   （我々は候補者を呼び入れます： ～を呼び入れる= send for/summon）
4. I (　　　　　) my sister.
   （妹を訪問しました： ～を訪問する= visit）
5. School was (　　　　　) because of heavy snow.
   （大雪のため休校になった： 中止する、取り消す=cancel）
6. I may (　　　　　) help.
   （助けを求めるかもしれません： ～を声をあげて求める= appeal for）
7. I will (　　　　　) a friend of mine tomorrow.
   （明日友達に電話します： ～に電話をかける= phone）
8. Elley (　　　　　) his house in the morning.
   （エリーさんは朝彼の家を訪問しました： ～を訪問する＝visit）
9. He (　　　　　) one of his classmates for help.
   （彼は助けをクラスメイトに呼びかけました： ～に呼びかける= speak to）
10. Give me a (　　　　　) whenever you need my help.
    （助けが必要な時はいつでも電話してください： 電話をかけること＝ring）

（語群）　called at,　called in,　called to,　call in,　called off,　called on,　call up,　call out for,　called for,　call

Part 2 Understanding Phrasal Verbs — 句動詞の理解 —

（奇数番号の解答）
1. called for,　 3. call in,　 5 called off,　 7. call up,　 9. called to

3. "Call" に関する「話の泉」

・ call you back と call back you どちらが正解でしようか。
次の例文から正解が分かりますよ。

「鈴木に折り返し電話をさせます」
① I'll have Mr. Suzuki call you back.
② I'll have Mr. Suzuki call back you.

　上記2文には2つのポイントがあります。最初のポイントは句動詞 call back の使い方です。例文①では 他動詞（call）＋代名詞（you）＋副詞（back）の語順になっており、例文②では他動詞（call）＋副詞（back）＋代名詞（you）の語順になっています。 back は副詞ですので、文中の位置は比較的自由です。それゆえ、①②どちらの位置に来ても OK です。しかし you が代名詞なので call と back の間に入ることになります。よって例文①が正解です。また、もし you の代りに Mr. Tanaka にすれば例文の①②どちらも正解となります。

◎　基本動詞 "Bring"

1. "Bring" の用法

　bring は他動詞で、come（自動詞）に意味が対応し、「外から中心へ～を持つ

UNIT 2　GRAMMAR

てくる／連れてくる」という意味です。

① bring ～ around ＝ ～を説得する

　I'll bring Ichiro around.　（一郎さんを説得するつもりだ）

② bring in ～ ＝ ～を入れる

　We need to bring in new members.（新しいメンバーを入れる必要があります）

③ bring out ～ ＝ ～を引き出す

　He brings out the best in me.　（彼は私の最良のものを引き出してくれます）

④ bring ～ to lie ＝ ～を再生する

　How can we bring this company to life?

　（この会社を再生するにはどうすればいいの）

⑤ bring up ～ ＝ ～を育てる

　I was brought up by my grandparents.　（祖父母に育てられた）

⑥ bring about ～ ＝ ～ を引き起こす

　Poverty brings about many social problems.

　（貧困が多くの社会問題をもたらす）

2. "Bring" を使用した句動詞／熟語の練習問題

Part 2 Understanding Phrasal Verbs — 句動詞の理解 —

問題： 日本文に合うように、次の"Bring"の句動詞／熟語の(　　)内に適切な語を次の語群から選び、英文を完成させなさい。

1. I hear the government is (　　　　　　　) new measures this month.
   （政府は今月新たな政策を立てるそうだ）
2. It (　　　　　　) the best in that actress.
   （それがその女優の一番良いところを引き出した）
3. I was born in the U.S., but (　　　　　　　) in Japan.
   （合衆国で生まれましたが、日本で育ちました）
4. The snow could (　　　　　　　) tree branches and power lines
   （雪の重みで木の枝が折れたり送電線が垂れ下がる恐れがある）
5. Let's see if it will (　　　　　　　) a change in their attitudes.
   （それが彼らの態度に変化を生じさせるかどうか見てみましょう）
6. The album (　　　　　　　　) my happy memories in my childhood.
   （アルバムを見て子供のころの楽しい思い出を思い出した）
7. Eating too much may (　　　　　　　) a heart attack.
   （食べ過ぎは心臓発作を引き起こすかもしれませんよ）
8. Please (　　　　) the car (　　　　　　) by next week.
   （来週までに車を返してください）
9. That will (　　　　　　　) at least a few million yen in a year.
   （それは年間少なくとも数百万円の利益をもたらすだろう）
10. We should (　　　　　) Mary (　　　　　　) reality.
    （メリーを現実に引き戻すべきだ）

（語群）　bring about,　　bring ～ back ,　　brought out,　　bring ～ back to,　bringing in,　　brought up,　　bring on,　　brought back,　　bring in,　　bring down

UNIT 2　GRAMMAR

（奇数番号の解答）
1. bringing in,　　3. brought up,　　5. bring about,　　7. bring on,
9. bring in

3.　"Bring" に関する「話の泉」

　次のようなことを言いたい時に、日本語から直訳して、間違った表現をしてしまうことがあります。
○：正しい表現　　×：間違った表現　　△：別の意味／あまり使わない表現

「気持ちが悪いです」
　○　I feel sick.　　　×　I feel bad.　（何か失敗して後悔している時なら OK）

「頑張ってください」
　○　Take it easy.　　×　Work harder.　（もっと努力しろ）

「私はポジテイブ思考です」
　○　I'm a positive thinker.　　×　I'm positive.　（確信がある）

「これを試着してもいいですか」
　○　Can I try this on?　　×　Can I wear this?　（これを着て帰ってもいいですか）

「京都の良い想い出があるんです」
　○　I have good memories of Kyoto.　（京都には良い想い出があります）
　△　I have a good memory in Kyoto.　（京都では記憶力が良いのです）

「彼女は年配です」
○ She's a senior.　△ She's old.（年を取っていて、何もできないイメージ）

IV. 基本動詞を含む重要な句動詞／熟語

1. "Keep" を使った句動詞／熟語

keep a promise	約束を守る
keep a record	記録しておく
keep down ～	～を沈める
keep ～ from …	～を…させないようにする
keep on ～	～し続ける
Keep to the left.	左側通行。
keep in touch	連絡を取る
keep up with ～	～に遅れないようにする

2. "Do" を使った句動詞／熟語

You did it.	やったね。
Well done.	よくやった。
What do you do?	ご職業は何ですか。
Will you do me a favor?	お願いがあるのですが。
do away with ～	～を捨てる、～を廃止する
do over ～	～をやり直す
do up ～	～の手入れをする

do with ～	～でどうにかする、～で満足する
do the dishes	皿を洗う
do one's hair	髪を整える

3. "Make" を使った句動詞／熟語

make out ～	～を理解する、～を作成する、～を書く
make up	化粧する、を作りだす、を構成する
make up one's mind	決心する

4. "Take" を使った句動詞／熟語

Take it easy.	気楽にやって。
take up ～	～を始める
take over ～	～を引き継ぐ
take ～ for …	～を…と思う
take after ～	～に似ている
take care of ～	～の世話をする
Take care.	気をつけて。
take out ～	～を持ち出す
take off	を脱ぐ、離陸する

5. "Get" を使った句動詞／熟語

get married	結婚する
get tired	疲れる

get through	終える、通り抜ける
get over ～	～から回復する、～を乗り越える
get up	起きる
get down to ～	～に取りかかる
get away from ～	～から逃れる
get along	どうにかやっている
get off ～	～から降りる
get on ～	～に乗る
get in ～	～に乗りこむ、～に入る

6. "Have" を使った句動詞／熟語

have a bath	入浴する
have a rest	ひと休みする
Have a good time.	楽しんでください。
Have a nice day.	良い一日を。
have ～ on	～を着ている

7. "Go" を使った句動詞／熟語

Go for it!	がんばれ!
go after ～	～を追いかける
go along with ～	～に賛成する
go on	続ける、続く
go over ～	～に目を通す
go through ～	～を調べる

go out	出かける
Go ahead.	(お先に)どうぞ。

8. "Come" を使った句動詞／熟語

come from ～	～出身である
come across ～	～に出くわす
come along	うまくやっている
come out	現れる
come down with ～	(病気など)にかかる
Come on!	さあ行こう! さあ来い!
How come ～ ?	どうして ～ ?

9. "Give" を使った句動詞／熟語

give up	あきらめる
give off ～	～を発する
give in ～	～を提出する、屈服する
Give me a chance.	チャンスをください。
give a reply	返事をする
give a cry	叫ぶ
give a party	パーティーを開く
Give me a hand.	手伝ってください。
Give me a call.	電話してください。

10. "See" を使った句動詞／熟語

See you later.	じゃあ、あとで。
See you again.	じゃあ、また。
See you then.	じゃあ、その時に。
See you soon.	またね。
see 〜 off	〜を見送る
see through 〜	〜見通す
see about 〜	〜について考えておく、〜を処置する
Let me see.	ええっと。
I see.	なるほど。

11. "Put" を使った句動詞／熟語

put up with〜	〜を我慢する
put out 〜	〜を消す
put on 〜	〜を身につける
put off 〜	〜を延期する
put down 〜	〜を書き留める
put away 〜	〜を片づける、〜を蓄える
put aside 〜	〜を片づける、〜をわきへ置く、〜を蓄える

V. 句動詞によく使用される基本動詞

1. Eat   2. Fall   3. Feel   4. Fill   5. Find   6. finish   7. Fix
8. Fly   9. Get   10. Give   11. Go   12. Have   13. Keep   14. Know
15. Leave   16. Listen   17. Live   18. Lock   19. Look   20. Lose
21. Carry   22. Catch   23. Clean   24. Close   25. Come   26. Cut
27. Do   28. Draw   29. Drink   30. Drive   31. Ask   32. Back   33. Be
34. Blow   35. Break   36. Bring   37. Build   38. Burn   39. Buy
40. Call   41. Make   42. Open   43. Pay   44. Put   45. Run   46. See
47. Send   48. Sign   49. Sit   50. Speak   51. Stand   52. Stay
53. Study   54. Talk   55. Tell   56. Throw   57. Turn   58. Wait
59. Walk   60. Watch   61. Write   62. Move   63. Pass   64. Play
65. Read   66. Say   67. Sell   68. Set   69. Sing   70. Sleep   71. Spend
72. Start   73. Stop   74. Take   75. Teach   76. Think   77.Try
78.Work   79. Use   80. Want

あとがき

　アメリカ人作家 Lena Clem 氏と筆者との出会いが本書成立の契機であるが、筆者がずっと抱いている思いを短編小説（From the Future）にする機会ともなった。さらに、前著である『Cross-cultural Studies through English ― 異文化学のすすめ ―』（ふくろう出版）でも共同執筆をしていただいた親交の深い、岸上英幹氏の英文法に対する深い造詣を披露する機会ともなった。

　本書が成立する上で、Tara Porczek 氏、Victoria Warne-Lang 氏、愛知産業大学の学生であった川村知美さん、中村美香さん、娘の関西大学の学生であった西田彩祐梨、ふくろう出版の亀山裕幸氏ほか、多くの人々のご協力をいただいた。この場をお借りして謝意を表したい。本書をきっかけとし、英書を含め英語に、多くの人々がより一層興味を抱いてもらえるようになることは、筆者の望外の喜びである。

執筆箇所

西田一弘：　本書の使い方／UNIT 1　From the Future・英語説明・QUESTIONS／あとがき

Lena Clem：　UNIT 1　The Farmer's Daughter・The Spoiled Child・From Stars・The Gold Coin・The Gift・The Fox and the Rabbit

岸上英幹：　はじめに／UNIT 2　GRAMMAR
　　Part 1　Understanding Prepositions　― 前置詞の理解 ―
　　Part 2　Understanding Phrasal Verbs　― 句動詞の理解 ―

Tara Porczek：　UNIT 1　Trees

録音： Victoria Warne-Lang、西田一弘
編集： 西田一弘
表紙デザイン： 中村美香

執筆者紹介

西田一弘： 愛知産業大学短期大学 国際コミュニケーション学科 准教授
岸上英幹： 明治大学 リバティアカデミー講座 講師
Lena Clem： アメリカ人作家
Tara Porczek： カナダ人作家

JCOPY 〈(社)出版者著作権管理機構 委託出版物〉

本書の無断複写(電子化を含む)は著作権法上での例外を除き禁じられています。本書をコピーされる場合は、そのつど事前に(社)出版者著作権管理機構(電話 03-5244-5088、FAX 03-5244-5089、e-mail: info@jcopy.or.jp)の許諾を得てください。
また本書を代行業者等の第三者に依頼してスキャンやデジタル化することは、たとえ個人や家庭内での利用であっても著作権法上認められておりません。

Modern English Fairy Tales
― 現代の英語おとぎ話 ―

2015年3月20日　初版発行
2018年11月10日　第2刷発行
2021年1月31日　第3刷発行

編著者　　西田　一弘

著　者　　Lena Clem
　　　　　岸上　英幹

発　行　　ふくろう出版
　　　　　〒700-0035　岡山市北区高柳西町1-23
　　　　　　　　　　友野印刷ビル
　　　　　TEL：086-255-2181
　　　　　FAX：086-255-6324
　　　　　http://www.296.jp
　　　　　e-mail：info@296.jp
　　　　　振替　01310-8-95147

印刷・製本　友野印刷株式会社
ISBN978-4-86186-637-1 C3082 ©NISHIDA Kazuhiro, Lena CLEM, KISHIGAMI Hidemasa 2015

定価はカバーに表示してあります。乱丁・落丁はお取り替えいたします。